MISSION -

VIOLENCE
and
RECONCILIATION

Papers read at the biennial conference of the British and Irish Association for Mission Studies at the University of Edinburgh June 2003

Editors
Howard Mellor & Timothy Yates

CLIFF COLLEGE PUBLISHING

ISBN 1 898362 32 7

British Library Cataloguing in Publication Data.
A catalogue record for this book is available from the British Library.

Cliff College Publishing,
Calver, Hope Valley, Nr Sheffield S32 3XG

Printed by:
MOORLEY'S Print & Publishing
23 Park Rd., Ilkeston, Derbys DE7 5DA
Tel/Fax: (0115) 932 0643

from data supplied on disk

CONTENTS

III. RECONCILIATION IN ECUMENISM AND INTER-FAITH RELATIONS

CONTRIBUTORS

Cecelia Clegg serves on the staff of the Irish School of Ecumenics. She is co-author of *Moving Beyond Sectarianism: Religion and Conflict in Northern Ireland.*

Kenneth Fleming is Theological Tutor at the Theological Institute of the Scottish Episcopal Church in Edinburgh.

Drew Gibson is a Presbyterian Minister who teaches at Belfast Bible College.

Jacques Matthey is Editor of the *International Review of Mission* and Co-ordinator of the Mission and Evangelism Team of the World Council of Churches.

David Porter is Director of ECONI (Evangelical Contribution in Northern Ireland).

Margaret Raven is an Anglican Priest who has served in Nicaragua and is currently working in the Scottish Episcopal Church.

Kenneth Ross is General Secretary of the Board of Mission of the Church of Scotland with experience of Malawi.

Robert Schreiter is Vatican II Professor of Theology at the Catholic Theological Union, University of Chicago, and Edward Schillebeeckz Professor of Theology and Culture at the University of Nijmwegen, The Netherlands. He is the author of *Reconciliation: Mission and Ministry in a Changing Social Order*.

Andrew Wingate is Director of Inter-Faith Relations and Canon Theologian of the Anglican Diocese of Leicester. He has served in South India and is a recent Chairman of BIAMS.

The British and Irish Association for Mission Studies is an inter-confessional body founded in 1990 as a forum for both academic teachers and missionary practitioners and others interested in mission.

It publishes a twice-yearly newsletter and holds day conferences and biennial residential conferences.

Details of membership can be obtained from the Secretary,
C/o The Henry Martyn Centre,
Westminster College,
Cambridge CB3 0AA
or from the website
http://www.martynmission.cam.ac.uk/BIAMSConf.htm

BIAMS

FOREWORD

An important staging-post on the way to the production of this book came as an inspired idea for a day conference in Birmingham, 'Faith in the world after September 11th'. The inspiration came from Canon Andrew Wingate, then chairman of the British and Irish Association for Mission Studies (BIAMS), who suggested a meeting on 11 September 2002, one year on from the destruction of the twin towers. Some eighty people were attracted to the Carrs Lane Church Centre, where a platform of main participants included Imam Ibrahim Mogra, Rabbi Dr. Margaret Jacobi, Dr. Hardad Desai (a Hindu, originating from South Africa), Canon Wingate himself and Professor Anton Wessels of the Free University of Amsterdam who made the main presentation, the whole meeting chaired by Bishop John Austin, Anglican Bishop of Aston. Those present were confronted with such questions as 'who calls who a terrorist?'; 'is our faith in justice or did the twin towers rather represent western faith in economics, in Mammon rather than in Abba?'; 'does terrorism issue from poverty or even more fundamentally from exclusion?'; 'how committed are we to striving for justice if we wish for an end to terrorism?'. The Imam, faced with a general condemnation of Muslims for the events of September 11th, had to ask: were all Christians to be held responsible for the activities of Hitler?

Again, how were responsible people in the Muslim community to address young Muslims confronted by violence and provoked to violent responses? The Rabbi, too, told of an increase in anti-Semitic attacks since the event, bringing with them a sense of isolation and vulnerability for Jews. Canon Wingate struck a note of hope. His experience of inter-faith work in Leicester led him to discern a greater openness among Moslems and more positive attitudes to religious pluralism: the challenge for him was dealing with rhetoric from the USA. Professor Wessels pointed to the choice between confrontation and symbiosis: Sarajevo had in the past been an example of the latter with mosque, synagogue and Orthodox church in close proximity. Since then, as a kind of symbol of present ills, the bridge which was a jewel of Ottoman art had been bombed and destroyed by so-called Christian civilisation. He feared that anti-Semitism in the west was being replaced by anti-Islamism. So often the real issues were not religious differences but human inequalities.

John de Gruchy, in his Hulsean Lectures at Cambridge of 2002, published since as *Reconciliation: restoring justice* (SCM 2002), asked the crucial question: how do we speak of reconciliation? That is, given the depth of pain and injustice revealed by such examples as the Truth and Reconciliation Commission in South Africa, attempts to recover the 'disappeared' in Argentina or accounts of atrocities in Ruanda or Northern Ireland, glib resort to such language can be too easily an escapist pietism. The late Professor Adrian Hastings once expressed this vividly in a lecture in Harare in 1985 when reflecting on oppression and apartheid in the then context of South Africa: 'how can I be reconciled when someone is on my back and beating me?' John de Gruchy, coming out of the crucible of that South African experience has given a piece of living theology, based on the understanding of restorative justice, which at its best *can* lead to forgiveness and reconciliation.

Members of BIAMS who attended their residential conference at New College, Edinburgh in June 2003, 'Reconciling Mission, overcoming Violence', were privileged to hear another theologian who has reflected profoundly on these issues in Professor Robert Schreiter. Like de Gruchy, his has been no detached stance. He has acted as a kind of theological trouble-shooter in contexts across the world and his theology of reconciliation has been informed by personal involvement in crisis, as well as by reflection on scripture and tradition. His opening three lectures were rich fare for those seeking a satisfactory theology of reconciliation in the present setting of violence. John de Gruchy had referred appreciatively in his book to the work of Cecelia Clegg and Joe Liechty *Moving beyond Sectarianism: religious conflict and reconciliation in Northern Ireland* (Dublin 2001). The present volume has been greatly strengthened in its theme of violence and reconciliation by the rooting of the discussion in a particular field by Cecelia Clegg, David Porter and Drew Gibson, one every bit as demanding for the churches as South Africa and with the same confusing contrasts of genuine achievements towards reconciling initiatives and equally troubling failures to confront the challenges in their own membership and beyond. Although to some degree Northern Ireland predominated, other contexts in desperate need of reconciliation in Africa, Nicaragua, among British Asians and in inter-faith experience of Buddhism were also explored in the conference and are reflected in the contributions here. Jacques Matthey, editor of the *IRM*, gave a masterly overview of the place of reconciliation as a key element in the church's overall mission and of the *missio dei* itself from the perspective of one deeply involved in the WCC and its approach to inter-faith dialogue.

Examples can be found in the modern world of both Christian communities and individuals making decisive interventions in reconciliation. John de Gruchy gives the example of the San Egidio community in Italy, which used its influence to bring the civil war in Mozambique to an end in 1992. Beyers Naude's sermon of 1962, when he dissociated himself from Dutch Reformed Church attitudes on apartheid; and the role more recently of Desmond Tutu as chairman of the TRC toward restorative justice, are individual examples. J. D. Gort has written: 'impunity, with its denial of the verifiable truth and refusal to allow the healing of the memories, ticks away like a time bomb in the midst of societies' (*Mission Studies* XIX, 2, 2002, pp. 104-5). For de Gruchy, the biblical notion of the covenant is fundamental in the attempt to keep justice and love in balance, making justice relational and social: 'God's justice, power and love are reconciled in the fact that the just dies for the unjust, thereby justifying and embracing the ungodly in a new covenantal relationship' (p.204). There is nothing glib here nor any of the 'cheap grace' so rightly criticised by Dietrich Bonhoeffer. Reconciliation has to be based on truth-telling, which can be a very painful process for both the perpetrators of evil and the victims. As Genevieve Jacques has written: 'the conscience of humankind on the threshold of the third millennium remains haunted by mass and systematic crimes which have escaped judgement and which leave in the memory of the traumatised victims and peoples a permanent scar which time cannot remove. So long as there remains a feeling that a great injustice has not been put right ... when the present is unworthy of the past, the future will soon take revenge'. (*Beyond Impunity: an ecumenical approach to Truth, Justice and Reconciliation* (WCC, 2001)).

We hope that this third BIAMS volume in succession to *Mission – an Invitation to God's Future* (Cliff College, 2000) and *Mission and Spirituality: creative ways of being Church* (Cliff College, 2002) will provide for serious reflection on issues of profound significance for the future of the church and of the world.

Howard Mellor
Timothy Yates

Part I

RECONCILIATION AND PEACE MAKING

THE THEOLOGY OF RECONCILIATION AND PEACEMAKING FOR MISSION

Robert Schreiter

Introduction: Change of Context, Change of Paradigm

Changes which have happened in the world since 1990 inevitably cause us to reflect on changes in the conduct of Christian mission. In his epic book, *Transforming Mission*, the late David Bosch already had a sense that major shifts were afoot. He concluded his survey of the history of Christian mission with what he termed "an emerging ecumenical paradigm."[1] What he gathered together in that paradigm was a list of what many of us would call *desiderata* for any future theology of mission. But it was in many ways a list without a clear inner coherence.

More than a decade later, we are in a different position to perhaps be able to speak more effectively to what shape a paradigm of mission might take. In the period immediately after Bosch finished his manuscript, a number of events pointed us in a somewhat different direction for the immediate future. Let me try to enumerate some of them here:

1. The national security states and civil wars in Central and Latin America countries nearly all came to an end or some kind of resolution. This was, of course, something to be welcomed by all of the world. But it left many

---

1 David Bosch, *Transforming Mission. Paradigm Shifts in Theology of Mission* (Maryknoll, NY: Orbis, 1991), chapter 12.

countries in that part of the world exhausted and traumatized by recent events. The reconstruction of societies after a long period of war or totalitarian rule challenged those who would lead the societies to a new place. Often overt conflict had ended, but powerful military regimes were still in place. The impoverishment which most nations faced did not portend well for the future. The theologies of liberation, which had been honed so well to resistance of oppression, had found oppressive conditions still to be present among the poor and marginalized, but the conditions under which they were to be addressed had shifted dramatically.

2. The collapse of the Berlin Wall in 1989, and the end of the Soviet bloc of influence shortly thereafter led to a widespread ideological realignment of the world. Marxist states still existed, but Marxism as a prescription for a better society was fundamentally discredited. How these formerly Communist societies were to be reimagined became a major challenge. Two other events were at least partially constituted by the end of the bipolar ideological and political status of the world. First of all, economic and social globalization quickly rushed in to fill the ideological void caused by the end of the bipolar political and economic order. It presented itself, through neo-liberal forms of capitalism and the power of social media, as having no alternative to itself. One was either included or excluded. The sweep of globalization led to further dislocation in already challenged societies. Second, the end of the bipolar grip on the political order allowed both for the emergence of many new states and for the (re) assertion of ethnic identities. The number of armed conflicts in the world surged in the early 1990s. However, most of these conflicts were now within national boundaries rather than across political borders. The number of conflicts has abated somewhat in the first decade of the new century, but there are still many "hot" situations in the world today. Picking up the pieces in those societies will consume energies for decades to come.

3. Globalization produced other effects as well. The commemoration of an earlier phase of globalization - the five hundredth anniversary of the first voyage of Christopher Columbus - prompted a review of colonization by the European and later North American powers, and its effects on indigenous peoples around the world. Calls for reparation and the healing of memories punctuated these encounters, as memories of painful pasts were brought again to the fore.

4. One final aspect of globalization might be mentioned as well. Typical of a period of globalization is an increase in the relative ease of travel. Migration is once again a major fact of contemporary life. Previously homogeneous societies frequently now find themselves suddenly, and profoundly, multicultural. With few exceptions (such as South Korea), this is now a fact of societies today.

5. The end of apartheid rule in South Africa focused the world's attention on the evils which had occurred there, but also on the plight of much of the African continent today. The continuing prevalence of poverty, the disruption of civil wars, brutish rule and corruption, the debilitating effects of HIV/AIDS, and inattention by the wealthy world to other pandemic diseases in that part of the world make for a sad and sorry picture of much of Africa today.

6. The pressures of modernity and globalization have also led to an upsurge of interest in religion throughout the world. Even though the pundits of secularization had predicted that, following the European model, religion would first be privatized and then steadily fade away, the world today in most areas is more religious than it was before. This is not necessarily good news, however. A salient feature of this new interest in religion is the rise of various forms of fundamentalism, at times linked with political violence. Pentecostalism, the fastest growing form of Christianity in the world today, is seen with a greater ambivalence on the world scene. On the one hand, it represents the agency of the poor who are struggling to take some hold of their own lives. On the other, it can be an escape from the dreary prospects which await most of the poor in the world today.

This dire litany of issues provides something of a picture of the state of much of the world and the world's population in the first decade of the twenty-first century. I present this not to paint a sombre picture so that we can counter it with a cheery Good News of Salvation. I do it rather in order to remind us of the depth of suffering in the world today, and some of the challenges we will face. The last decade has made us all keenly aware of the depth and strength of violence in our world today. Prospects in the immediate future do not harbour much hope for change. Take, for example, the question of median age. No European country is replacing its population because of low birth-rates. Thus, European societies are ageing, both because of lower birth-rates and because of greater longevity. The recent battles over pension funds are only the beginning of the social challenges in that part of the world. Part of the upsurge of violence in the poorer parts of the world has to do with having a young, frustrated (male) population, who statistically (at least historically) are more prone to violence. Those involved in the violence of September 11, 2001 in New York and Washington were nearly all younger than thirty. When one sees the increase of child soldiers in parts of Africa and Latin America, one sees what possible consequences may lie ahead for a world which does not take care of its young nor offer them opportunity.

The rise of terrorism in recent years and the greater awareness of violence across the board, due in part to the reach of the global media, make ending violence and the rebuilding of societies after violence a major priority for the world today. The coupling of violence with religion can give violent behaviour even greater virulence. It is not surprising, then, that there is such interest in how to end violence (witness the World Council of Churches' decade-long program to end violence) and how to ensure peacemaking. Ten years ago, with the end of major nuclear threat, some people opined that peacemaking might become an obsolete undertaking. No one would say that today.

So we now find ourselves with a keen interest in themes like ending violence, peacemaking, and reconciliation. As the theme of this BIAMS meeting, it will be examined from a variety of different perspectives. In this series of lectures, I wish to explore especially how ending violence, peacemaking and reconciliation are creating for us the need for a new paradigm in mission. As was said at the outset, Bosch's magnum opus on mission was completed before many of these tumultuous events described here had begun to unfold. Today, we can take up his challenge to rethink a paradigm for mission in the first part, at least, of this new century.

In this first presentation, I want to propose a theology of reconciliation as such a paradigm for mission in a time so deeply concerned with ending violence, with peacemaking, and with rebuilding of societies. I wish to do this by proposing a theology of reconciliation which I find in the Pauline writings of the New Testament, and then suggesting how these elements of a theology of reconciliation can inform a way of conducting Christian mission. In order to achieve this latter end, I will try to situate a paradigm of mission as reconciliation in some of the other forms of mission which have emerged in the last fifty years.

A Theology of Reconciliation

The word "reconciliation" does not occur all that frequently in the Bible, but the idea of reconciliation and the concern for it can be found in many places. Think, for example, of the moving stories in Genesis of Esau and Jacob, or of Joseph and his brothers. New Testament parables like that of the prodigal son are enshrined in the very centre of the Christian imagination. I would like to concentrate here, however, on the Pauline writings, especially 2 Corinthians 5 and Ephesians 2. There we have accounts which deal both with what might called "vertical reconciliation" (i.e., our relation to God), and "horizontal reconciliation" (i.e., our relation with one another). It seems to me that we need both of these dimensions to understand our task in mission today. To focus only on the vertical dimension (as would be the case elsewhere in Paul, such as in Romans 5) does not help us with the vexing situations of violence and the aftermath of violence in our world today.

I would sum up this theology of reconciliation in five points, based on Paul's writing in the two books just mentioned:

1. *Reconciliation is first and foremost the work of God.* Christians believe, of course, that salvation comes from God and not from our efforts. In thinking of reconciliation in that light, what becomes apparent - especially in social situations after conflict - is that the magnitude of the damage which has been done is ultimately beyond any human effort at correction. Only God has the perspective that can ultimately sort everything out. Thus, Christians

hold to the idea that it is God who through Jesus Christ brings about reconciliation, not ourselves. We are but agents of God's activity - "ambassadors for Christ's sake" in Paul's words in 2 Cor 5:20. For this reason, reconciliation is as much a spirituality for Christians as it is a strategy. It is only by living in communion with God that we can come to recognize the action of God toward reconciliation in our world. To assume that reconciliation is something which comes entirely from our efforts results in the psychological and physical burnout so common among those who work in post-conflict situations.

2. *God's reconciling work begins with the victim.* The common-sense understanding of reconciliation goes something like this: the wrongdoer repents of the wrongdoing and seeks forgiveness of the victim. The victim forgives the wrongdoer and then there is reconciliation. Laudable as this sense of reconciliation may be, there is a problem with this scenario: too often the wrongdoer does not repent. Sometimes the wrongdoer believes that nothing has been done wrong at all (think of the justifications given for totalitarian rule: to save the nation from subversive elements, and the like). In some instances the wrongdoer is no longer even present, and so cannot repent and seek forgiveness (Take for example the now deceased alcoholic parent whom the adult child wishes to confront). Where does all of this leave the victim? Is healing for the victim dependent upon the wrongdoer, and the wrongdoer's capacity to come to repentance? A Christian understanding would answer "no". Rather, God begins by healing the victim. This is done by restoring the humanity of the victim which had been wrested away in the act of wrongdoing. This is in line, first of all, with the Christian understanding of a God who looks out for the widow and the orphan, the stranger and the prisoner. The healing God works in the victims makes it sometimes possible for the victim to forgive the wrongdoer even before any repentance takes place. There was evidence of this in some of the testimonies made before the Truth and Reconciliation Commission in South Africa. Not all victims are able to do this, nor should undue expectations be placed upon them. But we have to

be able to account for how such forgiveness can and sometimes does take place without any action by the wrongdoer. I believe that this possibility reveals the very heart of the Christian understanding of reconciliation.

3. *God makes of both the victim and the wrongdoer a "new creation"*. To be healed of the trauma of the deed, or to be forgiven for what one has perpetrated, does not mean that things return to how they were before the conflict or the trauma arose. That would be to trivialize the extent of the damage that evil does. In both instances—healing and forgiveness - the victim and the wrongdoer find themselves in a new place, a place which they could not have anticipated. Healing comes as a surprise. Reconciliation is more than having the burden of the past lifted. It is the "new creation" of which Paul speaks in 2 Cor 5:17. For this reason, it is the vision of a new creation in the heart of the healed victim which provides the surest guide to reconstruction of a society after conflict. It provides a view which cannot be achieved by extrapolating from the *status quo ante* (how things were before the evil occurred), nor by imagining the symmetrical opposite of the evil now overcome.

4. *The Christian places suffering inside the story of the suffering and death of Christ.* Suffering is not of itself ennobling; by itself it is destructive of the human person. It is only when that suffering is brought into a new social space and with wider relationships that it can become ennobling and even redemptive. For Christians, this is done by placing their suffering within the framework of the sufferings of Christ. This is captured in another Pauline text, in Phil 3:10, where Paul says that he wishes to know Christ and be conformed into the pattern of Christ's death, so that somehow he, too, might come to know the power of Christ's resurrection. It is the belief in the power of the resurrection—a power which is more than the opposite of death, a power which comes from the living God—that makes the suffering more than the destruction of an individual person in society. For the Christian working toward reconciliation, such placing of one's own suffering in such a framework can help give meaning to otherwise meaningless suffering.

5. *Full reconciliation will happen only when God will be all in all.* The hymns at the beginning of the Letters to the Ephesians and to the Colossians remind us that any reconciliation we now experience will be incomplete. God is still working it out in Christ. This understanding, coupled with the first point about reconciliation made above (i.e., that God is the author of reconciliation) reminds us not to depend too much on our own capacities. We may experience frustration at how far the reconciliation we experience now can go, but we are hereby reminded that it is God who is our hope, drawing us forward even when things around us look utterly intransigent or even impossible. Here we experience the profound difference between optimism and hope: optimism arises out of our capacities and estimation of what we can do; hope comes to us from God, and provides a much broader horizon.

This, then, forms the heart of the Christian message of reconciliation as it is to be evidenced in the work of overcoming the consequences of violence in our world today. I would add something of a distinction between individual and social reconciliation. Individual reconciliation, as already noted, occurs when God restores the humanity, the human dignity, that has been wrested from a person in an act of wrongdoing. Social reconciliation (I am borrowing here from José Zalaquette, who chaired the Chilean Truth and Reconciliation Commission) is the moral reconstruction of society so that the wrongdoing of the past can never happen again.[2] The distinction between individual and social reconciliation is drawn here because there are different, though interlocking, dynamics at play. At the same time, I do not think that social reconciliation has much chance of succeeding if not led by a cadre of persons who have experienced the healing of individual reconciliation in their lives. It should be noted as well that the literature of conflict transformation will offer many other definitions. My purpose here is to focus on what might be the specifically Christian contribution to this discussion.

---

2 In Alex Boraine, Janet Levy, and Ronnell Scheffer (eds.), *Dealing with the Past: Truth and Reconciliation in South Africa* (Capetown, IDASA, 1994), 11.

Reconciliation as a Paradigm for Mission

If we take what has just been said about the Christian understanding of reconciliation, how might this inform a paradigm of mission? How might the work of reconciliation be seen as an embodiment or enactment of the Good News? We might best begin with a return to the Pauline corpus, this time to Ephesians 2:12-19. In this passage we have two parties, alienated from each other, being brought together and made a single body. The wall, which had separated them, has been pulled down. Now, together, they constitute a single group, fellow citizens in the household of God, alienated from each other no longer. This, it seems to me, forms the charter of a paradigm of mission as reconciliation.

How does this bringing together of groups once divided and far off into a single household translate into the conduct of mission? I would suggest that there are two dimensions to this, flowing from the definitions of individual and social reconciliation just offered above. Concretely, by engaging in the healing of the traumas of the past and by the moral reconstruction of a shattered society, the reconciling work of God is proclaimed and enacted in communities. Let us look at each of these two dimensions in turn.

Healing the Traumas of the Past

No matter how much one wishes to look to the future, the horrors of the past can impede any movement in that direction, and yawn before us like a bottomless pit. The past remains traumatic in some measure because there has been no opportunity to confront it and come to terms with it. In cases of civil conflict or repressive dictatorship, the wrongdoing of the past sometimes could not be voiced at all. In any event, the full emotional and spiritual impact of the past has not been plumbed. Without some measure of coming to terms with that past, the unhealed wounds will continue to fester, poisoning whatever new society is constructed, and posing the risk of victims themselves turning into the oppressors of others. How, then, are we to come to terms with the past? I would like to focus upon three areas to which Christian mission can contribute.

1. *Truth-telling*. The basis for healing the past is truth-telling. Truth-telling begins by speaking aloud those things kept hidden or secret during the conflict. People were often not allowed to speak of the atrocities they had experienced or witnessed in totalitarian regimes. One

could not raise the question of what had happened to loved ones taken away by the police or the armed forces. Speaking the truth breaks through the wall of silence imposed upon a society. It is one of the walls alluded to in Ephesians 2 which must come down. Second, truth-telling counters the falsehoods and lies perpetrated by the wrongdoers to legitimate their wrongdoing. The narrative created by wrongdoers is a narrative of the lie that is intended to replace any truthful narrative. It not only legitimates wrongdoing; it seeks to convince the victim that the lie can be the only truth about the victim. Truth-telling, then, is essential for creating a different kind of society. It also exonerates those who have lived under suspicion and false judgement (this is especially important for the families which have loved ones killed by the police or armed forces; the truth can now be told about what really happened). Third, truth-telling is a matter of trying to establish just what did happen, and equally importantly, why it happened. This is usually very difficult to ascertain, and in itself can take a long time. But without at least some attempts at it, a society cannot construct a new narrative about itself to replace the narrative of the lie which had reigned in the conflict. Hence the usefulness in some instances of Truth and Reconciliation Commissions. Such commissions must be constructed with an eye to just what a new society hopes to achieve. They may not be the best way in all circumstances.[3] Fourth, truth-telling becomes an important practice for the new society, something to be engaged in publicly and regularly. This is especially the case when untruthful propaganda has dominated public discourse.

2. *The Pursuit of Justice*. The truth must be told, but then it must be acted upon. Pursuing justice is both a way of healing the past, and of creating the practices which must undergird the new society. It must be remembered that truth-telling is a precondition for justice. To try to pursue justice without first establishing the truth runs the risk of

3 I have explored this in more detail in "Wahrheitskommissionen im Spannungsfeld von Wahrheit, Gerechtigkeit und Versoehnung," in Gerhard Beestermoeller and Hans-Richard Reuter (eds.), *Politik der Versoehnung* (Stuttgart: Kohlhammer, 2002), 227-240.

seeking revenge under the guise of justice. Revenge is another kind of falsehood, which only continues the violence of the past and does not overcome it. Basically, there are three kinds of justice that need to be pursued. The first is *punitive justice*. This entails legitimate authority ascertaining wrongdoing and then punishing those responsible for it. It is a necessary but limited form of justice. It is necessary because it is part of a public discourse acknowledging the wrongdoing of the past and stating publicly that such behaviour will not be tolerated in the future. But it is also limited as a form of justice. After a civil war, for example, not every combatant can be punished. To do so would require fair trials for each wrongdoer, and would tie up the resources and the emotional energy of a nation for decades. Thus there must be punitive justice, but it cannot continue indefinitely. Second, there is *restorative justice*. To the extent possible, whatever has been stolen must be returned, and those who have suffered loss must be given some compensation to aid them in the times ahead. The challenges here are many. Can property be restored to rightful owners decades after an oppressive regime is brought to a conclusion? Countries which have suffered through an extended conflict often do not have the resources to reallocate to their citizens. Even when this is the case, some public gestures must be made in this direction, however limited these might be. Third, there is *structural justice*. This involves changing the legal code, the judiciary system, and engaging in such acts as land redistribution, guaranteeing the rights of minority populations, and providing public services such as access to education, health, safety, and employment. This final kind of justice is part of the long work of reconstruction. It is in many ways the most difficult, but usually the most necessary.

3. *Healing of Memories and Forgiveness.* Healing memories and forgiveness are related to each other. Healing of memory does not mean forgetting what happened. To do so compromises one's own identity and integrity. Healing of memories means that the memories, though still present, are no longer toxic; that is, they no longer control

> our lives and poison everything they touch. Forgiveness has to be understood in this context. Forgiving is not forgetting; it is, rather, remembering in a different way. One is no longer controlled by the past event and by the perpetrator. One is able to see the perpetrator from a different perspective that does not allow the perpetrator to retain control over the victim. Forgiving the perpetrator need not entail not punishing the perpetrator or exacting restitution. To punish and to make restitution acknowledges the gravity of what has been done and the need for punitive justice. Nor does the victim have to befriend the perpetrator; such may not be possible or even desirable. In forgiving, the victim seeks the redemption of the perpetrator. It recognizes the human dignity of the perpetrator, however deeply twisted and flawed.

Healing the trauma of the past is complex and complicated, requiring the efforts and talents of many different kinds of people. What Christian mission brings to the process of truth-telling, pursuit of justice, and healing and forgiveness is not all that will be needed. But Christian concern for the truth, the truth which sets people free (Jn 8:32) comes from its experience of God drawing near. God's ways are ways of truth, and to live in truth is to live in God. The passion which Christians bring to the pursuit of truth can be an important resource in healing the past. Similarly, the pursuit of justice, much explored in the theologies of liberation in the twentieth century, can be a contribution to helping a society pursue justice, a justice which is not revenge, but a justice which emerges in right relationships between all in society. The pursuit of justice requires imagination, but also compassion. And finally the redemptive healing of memory and the engagement of forgiveness were cornerstone of Jesus' own ministry. Christians engage in healing processes because they believe that redemption is possible, and that only God is capacious enough to embrace the suffering which has happened. They believe too that the experience of healing which takes place in reconciliation is one of the most powerful experiences of the presence and action of God in the world which anyone can have. It is the Good News in the concrete. In looking at this dimension of a paradigm of mission as reconciliation, these elements speak perhaps most eloquently in deeds done rather than words given. They relate a pattern of relationships which begin to mirror the hoped for Reign of God.

The Moral Reconstruction of Society

The second aspect of reconciliation as a paradigm of mission is the moral reconstruction of society, that is to say, helping rebuild a society so that the evils of the past cannot be repeated. It is important here to focus on the *moral* reconstruction of society after a time of violence. This is not to be understood simply as preaching on moral values to be upheld. Rather, it means a special attention that must be paid to the steps that are taken in the reconstruction of society. As a society makes decisions about how it will move into the future, what does each of those decisions say about morals, norms, and values? What does the manner of the pursuit of justice say about the nature of justice in a just society? One might say that the moral reconstruction of a society has to do with attending to the symbolic reconstruction of society. What do our institutions, our policies, our actions say about us as a society? To be sure, the Christian Church cannot assume the entirety of the reconstruction of society, even if the majority of the population are Christians. But it does and can have some say about the nature of what a society does. It can do this not only in its engagement in the public discourse of rebuilding the society, but also in very concrete ways. Let me name a few.

1. It can create spaces of safety and trust in a society which has been until now unsafe and not trustworthy. In doing this, it creates an environment where the truth can be told, and where healing can be sought. That is why at times church property has been used as sites for working toward a new order in society. It can create environments where people can learn how to engage in public discourse - and disagreement - necessary to the fabric of civil society.

2. It can attend especially to the needs and interests of the victims. This is an outgrowth of the belief that God, too, begins with the victim in the healing process. In the competing voices in the process of reconstruction, it can be a voice for those who are not heard.

3. Most importantly, it can model the healing process which society itself needs. It can struggle to speak the truth about itself and its own role in the past; it can apologize; it can seek and extend forgiveness. This may be the most important things for the Church to do, and is a powerful form of witness.

4. It can offer a larger vision of the healing process. If the story of the Exodus was the master narrative for theologies of liberation, then the master narrative of reconciliation is the rebuilding of the ruined city, be that the rebuilding of Jerusalem after the Exile,[4] or the rebuilding of the household of God suggested in Ephesians 2. The narratives offered from Christian faith may not be able to be adopted by the entire society, but it is important for any society to have access to such narratives during a time of reconstruction. Such narratives not only allow one to see the bigger picture; they can also engender hope.

The moral reconstruction of society requires a sensitive moral compass, and commitment to honesty and humility. In those narratives of reconstruction, the Good News is communicated once again. The healing God can bring is on offer to those willing to seek it and those willing to live by its discipline. In this way, I believe, reconciliation - as healing of memories and as moral reconstruction of society - can constitute a paradigm for mission in a world which clearly needs it now so badly.

Reconciliation as Paradigm alongside Other Paradigms of Mission

In this third and concluding section, I want to try to situate what has been said here about reconciliation as a paradigm for mission alongside other paradigms of mission now salient in mission theory and practice. This will help us see the continuities and discontinuities between different forms of mission and practice.

At the outset it must be said that the peculiar shape mission takes is always influenced in some fashion by the larger Church's understanding of itself and its perception of the "other" to whom it is directed. Rereading Bosch's great work on mission, already referred to, makes that eminently clear. Context does not determine mission but mission in any given time and place cannot be understood without reference to context. Thus the mission motif of much of the European Middle Ages, "make them come in" (a reference to Luke 14:23 and the parable of the wedding feast) portrays a Christian Europe which sees itself at the centre of

4 This is the suggestion of Charles Villa-Vicencio in his *A Theology of Reconstruction. Nation-building and Human Rights* (Cambridge: Cambridge University Press, 1992).

the world, and the "others" which surround it as being on the periphery. The earth-shaking experience of the voyages of European discovery, from the end of the fifteenth century, required a profound reorientation of that vision. It was in the sixteenth century that Justinian von Welz proposed that the biblical motivation for mission should be Matthew 28:19-20, now known simply as the Great Commission. Rather than pressing others to come in, the imperative now was to go out.

I have suggested elsewhere (and the idea is not original to me) that another shift came in the middle of the twentieth century as the period of the great European empires came to an end. One place where that change was noted was at the 1981 SEDOS Mission Seminar, held near Rome. It brought over a hundred Roman Catholic missionaries, missiologists, and theologians together to reflect upon what was happening to mission now that the period of colonization was over. The end result of that seminar was a proposal that there were four forms of mission discernible in contemporary missionary practice. The first of these was proclamation. It had been the centrepiece of missionary thinking in the previous four hundred years, and continued to play an important, indeed indispensable role. But three new forms had emerged with the second half of the twentieth century, a time of independence from colonialism and nation-building. These forms were: dialogue, inculturation, and liberation of the poor.

Dialogue was most evident in the many interreligious dialogues which had come about since the middle of the century. Dialogue was not understood as an alternative to proclamation or a subterfuge to proselytize where proclamation was not possible. It was seen rather as an honest and soulful communication with the religious "other" which could lead to a deepening of commitment on both sides. Inculturation (or contextualization) began to emerge in both Protestant and Catholic circles in the 1970's as a new force. It gave greater voice to churches to express the Good News of Jesus Christ in their own idiom. It was not an historical accident that the initial interest in inculturation coincided with the efforts at nation building in the former European colonies. But the form of mission, which had perhaps the greatest impact on the missiological imagination, was the liberation of the poor. Starting in Latin America in the late 1960s, but quickly spreading to other continents, the concern for the liberation of peoples from poverty and oppression was a powerful vehicle for conveying the Good News that God stands especially by the poor.

If a biblical warrant for carrying out mission in this manner were sought, one might choose Luke 24:13-35, the Emmaus story, for models of dialogue and inculturation, or Luke 4: 18-19, the incident in the synagogue in Nazareth, where Jesus cites the passage from Isaiah 61, for mission as liberation.

All three of these forms which emerged in the twentieth century remain important modes of mission in the twenty-first. I think, however, that the events of the 1990s, chronicled at the beginning of this lecture, have all modified the valence of these models of mission. In the case of dialogue, there is clearly now a greater imperative to dialogue not just to get to know the religious other, but to form bonds of interreligious solidarity against the hijacking of religion to legitimate violence. An example might be useful here. When the war broke out in Bosnia, the leaders of all three of the major forms of faith—Muslims, Orthodox, and Roman Catholic - spoke out against the violence and the use of religious affiliation to legitimate that violence. None of the voices was strong enough to be heard. To make sure such things do not happen again, leaders of these three traditions have formed an Interfaith Council, which meets publicly and regularly so that, should violence happen again, they will be able to speak out and to be heard.

Inculturation has taken some new turns in the past decade as well. Certainly the leading consideration about inculturation in the first two decades of its pursuit was an issue of identity of the churches in the newly formed nations. One can detect some changes in the 1990s and in the present decade. Here one finds, on the one hand, a postcolonial retrieval of a deeper past and, on the other hand, an attempt to situate local identity in the midst of a wider picture and to use the voice which emerges to speak out for justice and equity in an age of globalization.[5] The early optimism about nation-building has been sobered by the effects of globalization, by the development of multicultural societies, and the struggle to envision a future.

---

5 These changing features are explored by Jan H. Pranger in his "Redeeming Tradition. Inculturation, Contextualization, and Tradition in a Postcolonial Perspective," (University of Groningen diss., 2003).

Liberation has received perhaps the widest attention in all of this. Given the opposition of the Vatican to theologies of liberation in Roman Catholic settings, the disappearance of an economic alternative to global neoliberal capitalism, and the need to move from resistance to reconstruction in societies, theologies of liberation have undergone a profound soul-searching, the outcome of which is still not entirely clear.[6] To be sure, poverty and oppression still abound. But how can they be best addressed in a globalized world, a world that seems to be breeding ever greater violence, especially against the poor?

One can discern continuities and discontinuities with each of these forms of mission. Dialogue becomes increasingly important in the emerging multireligious societies being created by migration. And, as already mentioned in the example of Bosnia-Hercegovina, it is imperative as a voice against religiously legitimated violence. For the sake of reconstructing societies, especially those riven by religious violence, dialogue becomes also a practice of reconciliation. To be sure, the great religious traditions have different understandings of reconciliation, and each will need to contribute its own understandings of reconciliation, forgiveness, and peacemaking if multireligious societies are to succeed as human societies. Dialogue, therefore, will need to be more than an academic exercise. The concerns of healing and of the reconstruction of societies will take increasing priority.

Inculturation, too, has a place in mission in the twenty-first century. But as was noted, its focus is undergoing change. Inculturation can be used ideologically to shut out other voices or create ethnicity where there was none before. One of the paradoxes of globalization has been that it homogenizes the world, on the one hand, but also leads to a new emphasis on the local, on the other. That new sense of the local must remain communicative, that is, serve as a bridge across boundaries of difference and not simply be a way of ignoring the other. The particular and the common, the local and the universal need all to have a voice in the twenty-first century. This latter is also a concern of reconciliation as a paradigm. Voices need to be heard in the authenticity which a peculiar locale can give them, but they

6 See for example the collection by Georges De Schrijver, *Liberation Theologies on Shifting Grounds. A Clash of Socio-economic and Cultural Paradigms* (Leuven: Uitgeverij Peeters, 1998).

must also be able to connect with other voices, both similar and dissimilar to their own.

Liberation, too, is a voice still needing to be heard. It continues to point to situations of suffering, even as it seeks an appropriate form to respond to them. The concerns of liberation as mission share with reconciliation are numerous.[7] Both are concerned with suffering and its alleviation; both pursue justice. Where there may be a difference may actually be one of emphasis. Liberation theologies, as they have developed, have been particularly good at creating resistance to evil and to engendering hope. Reconciliation theologies, as they are developing, focus more on the healing of societies after oppression and to the reconstruction of those societies. One of the things that is being discovered in many countries is that the skills needed to lead in resistance are not the same as those needed to create a common, shared approach to reconstruction. This may be emblematic of where the two theologies (and therefore, the two paradigms of mission) may be different.

Conclusion

This first lecture has tried to set out elements of a Christian understanding of reconciliation, and how that is translated into a new paradigm of mission. A final section looked especially at how this new paradigm of mission as reconciliation could be situated among three other paradigms that emerged in the second half of the twentieth century. As I hope can be seen, the emergence of reconciliation as a new paradigm of mission was prompted by the changes the world experienced through the 1990s. It builds upon a profound message of Christian faith, and draws upon three other paradigms which developed in time immediately before it did. What will be the enactment and the further resources for this paradigm, and how to prepare missionaries as agents of reconciliation, will be the topics of the next two lectures.

7 I have tried to work this out in more detail in "Liberation and Reconciliation as Paradigms of Mission," in *SMT: Swedish Missiological Themes/Svensk Missionstidskrift* (forthcoming).

THE SPIRITUALITY OF RECONCILIATION AND PEACEMAKING IN MISSION TODAY

Spirituality in Reconciliation and Peacemaking

When most people think about the concept of reconciliation, either on the individual or the social level, they are likely to expect a discussion of techniques of conflict transformation. There is, of course, an entire body of literature on conflict prevention, conflict management, and conflict transformation, much of which can be useful to the missionary.[1] Indeed, some of the findings and methods developed in this area will be discussed in the next lecture. While these have their legitimate place in the work of reconciliation and peacemaking, what I wish to focus on here is the role of a supportive spirituality for those who, as missionaries, work within a paradigm of reconciliation. I do this for two reasons. First of all, there is a greater interest in spirituality in the work of reconciliation and peacemaking today as a whole. One of the things which became evident in the 1990s, as interest in reconciliation began to grow, was that the burnout rate among those involved in reconciliation work was extremely high. The task of conflict transformation is arduous, and fails perhaps most of the time. It is always a lengthy process, demanding focus and commitment on the part of those involved. As this became clearer, many conflict resolution workers in secular non-governmental organizations (NGOs) began turning to their religious counterparts, especially in relief and development agencies, expecting to find some help from their spiritual traditions. Unfortunately, workers in those agencies had been caught unawares of the need to engage in reconciliation work as everyone else. They had often no more idea on how to draw on their spiritual traditions than anyone else. In the last six or eight years, a great deal more effort has been put by these agencies to discovering spiritual roots which can nourish

---

1 Two examples which are relevant to missionary work would be Carolyn Shrock-Shenk (ed.), *Mediation and Facilitation Training Manual. Foundations and Skills for Constructive Conflict Transformation* (Akron, PA: Mennonite Conciliation Service, 2000); *Peacebuilding: A Caritas Training Manual* (Vatican City: Caritas Internationalis, 2002).

this important but arduous work. Some experts in conflict resolution have themselves written about religious motivations for their work.[2]

Second, the focus here will be on the distinctive contributions made by missionaries (or one may want to broaden it to religious workers in general[3]) in situations of reconciliation and peacemaking. What missionaries do as missionaries is of central interest. Thus the spirituality must conform in some way to the theology of reconciliation out of which missionaries work.

This presentation will be structured as follows. It begins with a brief description of what is meant here by "spirituality," since this is a term that, until recently, was used mainly in Roman Catholic and Orthodox circles. Then a number of elements distinctive to this spirituality will be discussed. The elements presented here do not constitute the entirety of what such a missionary spirituality ought to be, since a spirituality flowing out of this paradigm of mission is still in the developing stages. Finally, an example of how this spirituality might be developed further will be presented, to show its links both to Scripture and to the theology of reconciliation set out in the previous presentation.

A Note on Spirituality

"Spirituality" is a term that, until recently, was used mainly in Roman Catholic and Orthodox circles. For many Protestants, it was even somewhat suspect as a Christian practice altogether. Spirituality seemed to be a certain set of practices one followed in obedience to some human authority, thereby restricting the freedom of the individual Christian. For many Roman Catholics too, it was seen as a set of prescribed, church-approved practices, connected with religious orders. Thus, one could speak of Franciscan or Carmelite spirituality, ways of living out the imperatives of the Gospel in those religious families.

But in recent years, the understanding of spirituality has broadened both theologically and culturally. A number of works have appeared over the past several decades on missionary

2 John Paul Lederach, *The Journey toward Reconciliation* (Scottdale, PA: Herald Press, 1999).

3 For the latter, see Mary Ann Cejka and Thomas Bamat (eds.), *Artisans of Peace: Grassroots Peacemaking among Christian Communities* (Maryknoll, NY: Orbis, 2003).

spirituality, i.e., specific forms of Christian discipleship connected with missionary activity.[4] The entry of South and East Asian religious traditions, such as Buddhism, into Western societies had an effect on the use of the term as well. In those instances, spirituality was often seen as a more apt word to use than theology, since the only purpose of doctrines or ideas are intended only as a springboard to enlightenment. The development of practices of non-violence led also to speaking of a spirituality as the ideas which informed such an approach to violence.

Most recently, "spirituality" has come to mean interest in the transcendent without commitment to any organized religious tradition. The phrase "I am spiritual, but not religious" echoes this attitude. While this will not be the meaning of spirituality as it is presented here, such usage has made the term "spirituality" more acceptable, at least in that part of the world.

What then do I mean by spirituality? I would define it for our purposes here as a distinctive and coherent set of ideas, attitudes, and practices which represent a way of living out the Gospel message. In terms of a spirituality of reconciliation, this would mean taking the theology of reconciliation as discussed in the previous presentation and translating it into a way of life and action for missionaries today. Looking back to some of the other paradigms of mission, with their attendant spirituality, might help clarify this.

In the medieval theology of mission, based on Luke 14:23 ("make them come in"), the parable of the wedding banquet, in which the host sends out his servants to bring in people from the highways and byways suggested a spirituality of reaching out to those living in ignorance of the Gospel, and bringing them in to the Church. In the theology of mission based on the Great Commission (Matt 28:19-20), the spirituality suggested was of someone going out from his or her homeland, and boldly proclaiming the Gospel. There was in this an image of missionary as hero or missionary as martyr, because of the hardships and opposition the missionary was likely to encounter. The theology of mission based on Luke 4 or Luke 24 in the second half of the

---

4 E.g., Michael Reilly, *Spirituality for Mission: Historical, Theological, and Cultural Factors for a Present-day Missionary Spirituality* (Maryknoll, NY: Orbis, 1978); Anthony Gittins, *Reading the Clouds. Mission Spirituality for New Times* (Ligouri, MO: Ligouria Publications, 2000).

twentieth century see the missionary as prophet (Luke 4) or as one who accompanies people on a journey.

If 2 Cor 5 and Ephesians 2 provide the biblical warrant for mission as reconciliation, then the missionary spirituality flowing from them bespeaks the missionary as one who overcomes alienation and is a peacebuilder. Bringing together what has been separated, healing memories of the past, and building a new city would be salient images here. To see how to move the theology of mission as reconciliation into a spirituality of reconciliation, we turn now to some of the ideas, images, and practices of such a spirituality.

Ideas and Images of a Spirituality of Reconciliation as Mission

In spirituality, ideas and images often merge. This should not be surprising, inasmuch as spirituality has to do with how to live out a particular Gospel ideal. I would like to explore one such convergence of an idea and image that has become important to articulating a spirituality of reconciliation as mission; namely, that of wounds.

When one thinks of the consequences of events that have forever changed the lives of individuals and societies in a negative fashion, the idea of wounds comes readily to mind. A wound is not only a testimony to the fact of something wrong having happened. Its perjuring character as wound or as scar witnesses to the role of memory in the process of trauma and recovery. A wound is often something which never entirely heals. It is a sign of a permanent change that has come about in the life of an individual and a society. Old wounds sometimes resonate with changes taking place in an environment, or with cognate wounds. Think, for example, of how a bone once broken will detect changes in the weather, or leap to awareness when we encounter other kinds of brokenness.

Wounds have a double significance in a spirituality of reconciliation. There are, first of all, the wounds of the victim, be that an individual or a society. They may gradually heal over time, leaving only a scar as a reminder of what has happened in the past. Or they may remain open, continuing to fester and to plague the ones who bear them. We certainly see the latter happening with both individuals and societies. Over generations a wound may heal. Or they may serve as a constant reminder of what happened in the past, as though it was yesterday. For example, in 1989 Slobodan Milosevic recalled to the Serbian people the battle of the Field of the Black Birds six hundred years previously, in which the Orthodox Serbs were defeated by the Ottoman Turks. The memory was salient enough to plunge the Balkans into war for the next six years. Memory of the medieval Crusades among Orthodox Christians and Muslims, the genocide of the Armenians by the Turks early in the twentieth century, of the Jewish Holocaust more than a half century ago function for other groups in the same way today. Memories can leap back to us as though the events were yesterday.

Wounds remind us that our lives have been altered forever. They reconstitute the past in the present, and can reorient our memories, placing the traumatic events of that past at the very centre of memory.

Wounds unattended to and allowed to fester can poison subsequent events. Too often have we seen how wounded individuals and societies go from being victims to themselves becoming perpetrators of wrongdoing toward others. One of the most difficult things to sort out in long-running civil wars is who is the victim and who is the perpetrator, since over time, the parties to the conflict have become both. Both claim their own victimhood as a warrant to inflict violence on the other party. Sometimes this happens in an overt manner that is unmistakable. In other instances it is harder to detect. I am thinking of situations where, after the ending of harsh oppression or totalitarian rule, a liberated society will turn to lawlessness and anarchy. Here unacknowledged wounds lead to the inflicting of new wounds on oneself or on one's society.

Secondly, there are the wounds carried by those seeking reconciliation. The wounds of individual victims or of victim societies cause a resonance to be set up in the wounds of those who would seek to bring about some resolution of these traumas. This is an area of woundedness that often does not receive the attention it deserves. The woundedness of the would-be healer has both positive and negative dimensions. From a positive point of view, a once-wounded healer can have a capacity for empathy with the victim that is not possible for the rest of us. Such a healer can enter the universe of pain and suffering that the victim is experiencing in a unique way. Such a healer can accompany the victim toward recovery in ways unknown to the rest of us. This is often most evident in the case of one-time victims, now healed, who as part of their healing receive a call or vocation to accompany others who have suffered similar traumas in the long and difficult path to recovery.

But the woundedness of the healer can have negative consequences as well. If the healer does not acknowledge the presence of his or her own wounds, either through inattention or denial, the healer's wounds can get in the way of helping others to overcome a painful past. This can happen in a number of different ways. Unacknowledged wounds can precipitate a victim into altruistic behaviour as a way of atoning for the wounds of the past. This can include not only a sense of "needing to be needed," but also an unwillingness to allow the person they are purporting to help to actually achieve any healing, lest the victim might no longer need the healer at all. The wounds of a healer can become a "hot button" (to use the American idiom) that, once pushed, simply gets in the way of a healing process. The healing process is diverted away from the victim and refocused upon the healer. Thirdly, the wounds of the healer may cause the healer to take undue risks, endangering both the healer and the victim.

I bring this potential problem up because it is not uncommon among missionaries. Sometimes they have gone out of their homeland in an attempt to escape their wounds, or prove something to themselves or to God. They may overcompensate in frenetic activity to prove to themselves that they are not wounded, or as some kind of reparation for the guilt of being wounded to God. I will return to a discussion of this in the next presentation.

Another potential negative consequence of unacknowledged wounds, especially in the case of efforts to heal wounded societies, is that wounds as vulnerable points in oneself can become the object of being assaulted in new ways. When one is confronted with the heinous conditions of genocide or mass killings, the deliberate maiming of individuals, the use of rape as a military strategy, one is, to so speak, staring evil directly in the face. Trying to undo the consequences of such evil can be construed as a kind of combat, a wrestling with evil incarnate. Whether one accepts a view of evil as personified in a figure such as Satan or not, the struggle against evil can engage all our powers, including our own personhood. The struggle can diminish our own humanity. (The psychological term for this is experiencing secondary trauma, that is, taking on unconsciously aspects of the trauma of the victims we are trying to help.) I have seen individuals who have not attended to their own wounds from the past who, in the midst of work for reconciliation, have begun to engage in questionable and even wrong behaviours that they themselves would otherwise stoop to doing. To put it in a perhaps over-simple way: if you don't protect yourself in struggling with evil, evil will attack your own wounds and "get" you.

To this point, the discussion of wounds may seem to have been primarily psychological or sociological. One might ask what this has to do with spirituality. Let me turn to that more explicitly now. One of the elements of a theology of reconciliation articulated in the previous presentation was that we cope with our suffering by placing the story of our suffering in that of the passion, death, and resurrection of Christ. Here is where what might be termed a psychology of woundedness meets theology: we place our wounds within the wounds of the tortured, crucified, and now risen, Christ. A biblical reference point here is John 20:19-29. In this story, Jesus presents himself to his disciples. Entering through a locked door, he appears in their midst and shows them his wounds. Exegetes have often interpreted this as a way of assuring the disciples that it is indeed Jesus of Nazareth who they are encountering. There is another reading of this act possible. Jesus appears in his glorified, resurrected body. The nature of this appearance is such (as we read from other accounts of the appearances in the Gospels) that the disciples do not recognize the appearance as Jesus, at least initially. Yet the phenomenon of the glorified body, signifying the transforming power of the resurrection, carries with it a profound paradox. This glorified body is capable of feats not possible for an earthly body, such as walking through locked doors. Yet this same transformed, glorified body still bears the signs of Jesus' execution and death - the wounds in his hands and in his side. Would not one presume that such ugly signs of the past would be erased in the act of transformation? Yet they are still plainly there on Jesus' body.

Perhaps these wounds should be understood in the manner in which wounds have been discussed here: namely, that the wounds of the past can never be entirely erased. We carry with us the memory of their pain because they signify how our lives have been irrevocably altered. Jesus may have been raised from death, but he still bears his earthly story of having been betrayed, arrested, tortured, and put to death. The wounds still present on his glorified body are eternal testimonies of that.

As wounds, these wounds on Jesus' glorified body carry with them a profound ambivalence. They can, on the one hand, be a burden that weighs us down as we go into the future. They have drawn us back into the suffering they signify and never allow us to come completely free of them. But on the other hand they can be a source of healing for others. And that is how they function in this particular story. They convince the disciples gathered in the upper room that the phenomenon they are seeing is indeed the Lord. Later on in the same story they heal Thomas. Thomas had been absent when Jesus first appeared to the disciples. The author of the Gospel of John focuses upon Thomas' incredulity when confronted with the story that Jesus had been raised from the dead. Again, another reading is possible. Perhaps Thomas felt excluded, left out because of not having been present at such a marvellous event. When Jesus confronts Thomas, Jesus invites him to touch Jesus' wounds - indeed, to enter them. Jesus' wounds become the means of reconnecting Thomas with Jesus, with the disciples, and even with himself. To echo another part of Scripture, "by his wounds we are healed" (1 Peter 2:24; Is 53:4).

By placing our wounds within the wounds of Jesus, by connecting our story with the story we can allow our wounds to become redemptive for others. This is phrased somewhat differently in the Letter to the Philippians (3:10), where the author speaks of being patterned into Christ's death, so that he might come to know the power of the resurrection.

A spirituality of reconciliation finds its salience in attending to wounds: the wounds of victims, the wounds of those working for healing, and the wounds of Christ. I will return to this idea in the third section of this presentation.

Practices of a Spirituality of Reconciliation as Mission

In this second section, I would like to turn to two practices that are part of a spirituality of reconciliation as mission: the place of contemplative prayer, and the creation of spaces of safety and hospitality.

Contemplative prayer might seem to be a practice that is at odds with being a missionary. Missionaries are, for the most part, incurable activists. They do indeed pray, but their prayer is more likely to be directed toward praise and thanksgiving, or to petition God for certain things. Why contemplative prayer? There are three reasons for making this suggestion.

First of all, contemplative prayer is intrinsically connected with the theology of reconciliation articulated in the first presentation. The cardinal point of this theology is that reconciliation is first and foremost the work of God, and we human beings are but agents of that reconciliation. For us to be faithful and effective agents of God's reconciliation we must take care to be in contact with God. Contemplative prayer seems especially suited to that. In contemplative prayer we find ourselves not taking the initiating or active role, but rather find ourselves waiting on God to speak to us. Such a role reminds us that we are but vehicles for God's reconciling action. We must be conformed to God if we are to be God's agents, "ambassadors for Christ's sake." (2 Cor 5:20) The waiting on God creates within us the stillness wherein we become capable of hearing God speak to us. Otherwise God's word to us runs the risk of being crowded out by our many words.

This waiting on God has other functions within a spirituality of reconciliation. The work of reconciliation takes great patience. When working with individuals, we must be prepared to hear the victim's story over and over again. Victims often need to tell that story of trauma, pain, and loss so many times in order to gain new perspective on it. Those involved in the work of reconciliation are called to accompany victims in that quest. For the most part that involves listening attentively and waiting until the telling of the story takes an unexpected turn. In situations of social reconciliation, patience is needed because the repair to a society takes a long time; it usually takes more than a generation before some measure of reconciliation is achieved. Again, this takes patience on the part of those involved in the reconciliation process.

This waiting which is cultivated in contemplative prayer has yet another function as well. Anyone who has practised contemplative prayer knows that our waiting on God to speak is not rewarded every time with a word. Sometime the waiting ends in waiting. One ends up experiencing, as it were, the absence of God. But experiencing this absence is of great value for the work of reconciliation. I have encountered on many occasions stories of those who have been tortured. One of the purposes of torture in its modern usage is to make the victim feel utterly alone. A refrain from torturers frequently recounted by victims is: "Scream as loud as you want. No one can hear you." I have encountered especially many people of deep faith who have said they always had believed that God would be with them, no matter what happened. But at the worst moments of torture, God was not there. All they experienced was a profound absence. Our waiting without hearing a word from God in contemplative prayer allows us, in some analogous fashion, to experience that troubling absence which victims can experience.

But the contemplative mode has other functions in a spirituality of reconciliation. Besides learning to wait on God, a contemplative posture makes it possible for us to contemplate our own wounds, to gaze upon them in unblinking fashion. We tend to want to avert our eyes from our wounds. Re-viewing our wounds reminds us of the pain of the past; it calls once again to our attention our weakness, our incompleteness, and literally our vulnerability. But as has already been noted, not to attend to our wounds makes us susceptible to blocking the way for reconciliation rather than facilitating it. Moreover, we can continue to learn from our wounds, as difficult as that may be. Encounters with new situations can bring with them new perspectives not only on the process of reconciliation, but also to the roles our own wounds can play in making reconciliation possible. Growing in the discipline of contemplation allows us to grow also in understanding the potential healing powers that our wound can have for others.

A third benefit of contemplation is that it can increase our capacity to imagine peace, the "new creation" of which Paul speaks in Second Corinthians (5:17). In working to overcome violence, peace is more than the cessation of conflict. It is rather a new state of being often quite different from what we had expected it to be. In seeking reconciliation, individuals and societies frequently imagine peace to be the *status quo ante*, a return to things as they were before the violence occurred. But of course we can never go back to that previous state. To be able to do so would mean that we would be able to undo and forget the harm that has been done to us. That harm's occurrence has irrevocably changed our potential future and us. It is seared in our memory. To extirpate utterly that memory would be to do harm to us once again. It would in effect be saying that what happened was not as important as we have made it out to be (thereby trivializing the event), or that we are not as significant as we have made ourselves out to be (thereby trivializing the victim). The key here to dealing with the harm of the past is not forgetting it, but remembering it in a different way, so that we regain some future and are not held hostage to the past. Contemplation provides us a way into the future by imagining things differently, moving beyond trying to create a symmetry between the future and the past. We can return here again to John 20: the glorified body of Jesus is not simply the resuscitation of his earthly body, nor is it utterly different. There is continuity with the past, but also wonderful new perspectives as well. So too will be the "new creation" toward which reconciliation beckons us.

Contemplation, then, is a key practice of the spirituality of reconciliation. It attunes us in a special way to God. It attunes also to ourselves as agents of reconciliation. And it attunes us to that new creation to which we are called.

A second practice of a spirituality of reconciliation I wish to explore briefly is the creation of safe and hospitable spaces. It is within these spaces that victims can dwell to explore their own wounds and come to imagine a different future. They are first of all *spaces*, understood as social spaces but as physical spaces as well. They are social spaces inasmuch as they are created by other human beings into a social environment where victims are not diminished further in their humanity. The physical space itself can contribute to the sociality of the space. Think for example of the law of sanctuary in medieval Europe: people could flee to churches and there be immune from arrest and prosecution. Truth and Reconciliation Commissions have at times found it useful to hold their hearings in churches in order to create the space for truth-telling and healing.

These spaces must first of all be safe. That is to say, they must be such that victims are not victimized a second time. The exploring of trauma, of harm done in the past is always risky. Such trauma is at bottom a profound breach of trust, a terrible disconnection from the pattern of human relationships. Healing is about the capacity to reconnect those sundered patterns of sociality. So victims must feel safe before they can confront the demons of the past. That sense of safety is one of the most important things that agents of reconciliation can mediate. It is in fact the first thing that those working in reconciliation must learn to do.

By mediating this sense of safety, agents of reconciliation prepare victims for an experience of the steadfastness of God; a God who does not abandon those God loves. This steadfastness is one of the principal characteristics of the God revealed in the Hebrew Scriptures. It is the basis of covenant, the relationship God forges with his people. It is that experience of steadfastness, of faithfulness, which creates the environment in which victims can again dare to hope.

Agents of reconciliation create these safe places by their capacity to be experienced by victims as trustworthy. This is largely achieved through the skills of communication of agents who work with victims. Agents who appear to be dependable, who do not recoil from the victim because of what has happened to the victim, who can be counted upon by the victim to accompany them, come what may, who know how to listen without interrupting the victim's attempts to tell the story, who (in the words of *The Book of Common Prayer*) can "watch and wait and weep" with the victim in the night: these agents manifest the skills needed to create a safe place.[5]

These social spaces must not only be safe, but also hospitable. That is, they have to be welcoming to the victim in an idiom that the victim can understand. Too often hospitality may be extended in the ways that the agents of reconciliation know how to effect, but they may not be able to be understood and embraced by the victim. This is especially the case when there is a cultural difference between the agent and the victim (which is most often the case for the missionary as agent of reconciliation). Besides culture, agents of reconciliation must learn what acts of hospitality might recall memories of betrayal or other forms of harm in the events of the past with which the victim is wrestling. The points of engaging in hospitality in the social space are several. Beyond the obvious point of enhancing the experience of safety for the victim, extending hospitality to the victim is another way of saying that the victim is a valuable and valued human being. Inasmuch as trauma

---

5 I describe this in more detail in "Entering the Healing Circle: The Practice of Reconciliation," in Stephen Bevans, Eleanor Doidge and Robert Schreiter (eds.), *The Healing Circle. Essays in Cross-Cultural Mission* (Chicago: CCGM Publications, 2000), 176-188.

diminishes the humanity of the victim, offering hospitality is meant to reaffirm the humanity of the victim. Thirdly, the experience of human hospitality prepares the victim for its divine counterpart, the experience Christians call grace. The experience of reconciliation is one of receiving a surprising, undeserved gift. The healing that takes place, as already noted, can be one of the most profound and direct experiences of God that people can have. The hospitality of agents can prepare the way for that.

Learning how to extend such hospitality has two dimensions. One is for the agent to recall the hospitality he or she has received in the past, and the experience of graciousness that accompanied that. Reliving those experiences of hospitality can help agents to be more effective in their own extending of hospitality. Second, the agent must learn what counts for hospitality for the victim. In individualist societies, hospitality is largely guided by rules of etiquette, by the things one does. In more collective societies, hospitality is about the ongoing quality of relationships, reaffirmed by the constant giving of gifts. Knowing when and how to offer hospitality that victims can understand and appreciate is central to a spirituality and a ministry of reconciliation.

Further Developments in a Spirituality of Reconciliation as Mission

In the previous two sections I have tried to outline some of the elements of a spirituality, of reconciliation in a paradigm for mission. In this final section, I would like to sketch some possible developments of this spirituality, especially in light of biblical texts. As an example, I will use another Pauline text in Second Corinthians (4:7-11):

> But we have this treasure in clay jars, so that it may be made clear that this extraordinary power belongs to God and does not come from us. We are afflicted in every way, but not crushed; perplexed, but not driven to despair; persecuted, but not forsaken; struck down, but not destroyed; always carrying in the body the death of Jesus, so that the life of Jesus may also be made visible in our bodies. For while we live, we are always being given up to death for Jesus' sake, so that the life of Jesus may be made visible in our mortal flesh.

This passage captures many of the dimensions of a spirituality of reconciliation. Reconciliation is a treasure, a gift from God, but one that is carried in clay jars, that is, within ourselves as frail human agents of God's work. Exploring the wounds that mark reconciliation and returning to the memories of which they are emblematic pull us through a welter of emotions: the experiences of being afflicted, perplexed, persecuted and struck down. But even in the midst of such experiences, a certain strength carries us through: we are not crushed, driven to despair, forsaken nor destroyed. Those who struggle on in the work of reconciliation will recognize these emotions in victims, but often times in themselves as well.

What is clear at the same time is that despite these adversities we are not brought low, because of the great treasure we carry within us. Paul notes the paradox that makes this possible: because we carry the death of the Lord in our bodies. The language here is significant. Many of the afflictions which cry out for reconciliation are inscribed on our bodies — either on our individual bodies, as in the case of torture; or on the body politic, in terms of political memory. Memories are not only intellectual or emotional; they are often profoundly somatic. The death of Jesus we carry as such a somatic memory: the burden of his own death inscribed on our bodies. In this way it is something that cannot be forgotten. The death of Jesus is a wound of memory that has many dimensions. It is a wound that lies at the heart of our being and changes our orientation to those things that we have suffered. It gathers in our sufferings, takes them upon itself, and gives them a transfigured meaning. The wound is such that we cannot turn away from it, or avert our hearts and minds so as to forget it. The wound draws our suffering to itself, but is itself not the centre of attention. Rather, it points beyond itself to the resurrection of Jesus, when wounds will be transfigured and become a means of healing.

Johann Baptist Metz has spoken of the "dangerous memory" of Jesus Christ,[6] dangerous because it is liberating, dangerous because the attempt to end the story of Jesus by blotting out his life only led to its explosion in another dimension. The healing grace of reconciliation, the life of Christ made visible in our bodies, has that

6 Johannes Baptist Metz, *Befreiendes Gedächtnis Jesu Christi* (Mainz: Matthias Gruenewald Verlag, 1970).

same dangerous and liberative potential. It is the difference between being struck down, but not destroyed. God's capacity to reconcile all things in Christ, to make "peace by the blood of his cross," (Col 1:20) unveils for us the connection between our wounds, the wounds of Christ, and the wounded heart of God who so loves the world.

Conclusion

The spirituality of reconciliation as mission is still in its early phases of development. It grows not only out of the theology of reconciliation articulated in the last lecture, but also out of the renewed concept of the *missio dei* which has come to the fore again in recent years.[7] In this renewed understanding of a concept of mission from the 1950s, emphasis is placed upon how the work of mission is first of all the action of God in the world, an action in which we participate. That mission is nothing less than God's reconciling the world to God's own self through the action of Christ and the Holy Spirit. By reflecting on this theme, the connection between reconciliation and mission becomes even clearer. There is a theological bond between reconciliation and mission that is more than the current contextual need for overcoming violence in the contemporary world. Reconciliation is a revelation of how God relates to the world, and how God sees the destiny of the world. I hope that the attempt to articulate some of the elements of that spirituality of reconciliation here — the role of wounds, the place of contemplative prayer, the creation of safe and hospitable spaces — will lead to further commitment to this paradigm as a way of imparting God's Good News for the world.

7 See for example Stephen Bevans, "Wisdom from the Margins: Systematic Theology and the Missiological Imagination," *Proceedings of the 56th Annual Convention of the Catholic Theological Society of America* 56(2001) 21-42; Robert Schreiter, "Mission for the Twenty-First Century: A Catholic Perspective," in Stephen Bevans and Roger Schroeder (eds.), *Mission for the Twenty First Century* (Chicago: CCGM Publications, 2001), 32-42.

PREPARING MISSIONARIES TO BE AGENTS OF RECONCILIATION AND PEACEMAKING

Communicating the Gospel in a New Context

Throughout history, Christian missionaries have configured their work according to different understandings of how best to communicate the Gospel If reconciliation and peacemaking constitute a significant paradigm for mission today, how must missionaries be prepared in order to carry out their responsibilities?

To answer that question, it might be best to begin with a brief reflection on how missionary preparation changed over the past century. This might have the added advantage of raising questions which at first may not be obvious but may nonetheless be significant in the new paradigm we are exploring here.

If one goes back to the nineteenth and first half of the twentieth century, preparation of missionaries typically encompassed two areas: language and auxiliary professions. Formal language training was something that evolved from being apprenticed to a native speaker to the setting up of special language schools to equip the missionary in local languages. Roman Catholic missionaries sometimes lagged behind in formal language preparation because the administration of the sacraments was in Latin throughout the Church, and in that area no new preparation was needed. But missionaries across the denominational spectrum provided special service in the area of language by sometimes compiling the first grammars and dictionaries in local languages, thereby saving some of these from extinction.

Likewise, auxiliary professions took on importance. To the extent that Christian mission at the time of colonial expansion was often seen as a "civilizing" mission as well, education and Western medicine were prime and prized auxiliary professions. This was especially the case for women in many instances. Missionaries not only saw such things as education and healthcare as additional benefits for their charges, but also could point back to the Apostle Paul and his tent-making as a way of supporting himself.

The emergence of dialogue and inculturation as modes of mission in the second half of the twentieth century brought new perspectives on preparation of missionaries. Knowledge of other religious traditions became increasingly important, especially in Asia and Muslim areas of Africa. Any knowledge acquired earlier (with some exceptions) was used to combat or refute the great traditions. As dialogue became more important, the desired knowledge enabled the missionary to be able to collaborate more with other religionists. Around the same time, the importance of culture as a concept began to take hold across the denominational spectrum. Rather than presuming the superiority of Western culture, attention now focused upon the integrity of the cultures that the missionary encountered, as well as their preservation as a vehicle for expressing Christian faith. The heightening of importance of local culture in the immediate period following political independence made this commitment to culture even stronger. On the Roman Catholic side, the Second Vatican Council endorsed the concept of culture officially in its Constitution on the Church in the Modern World, *Gaudium et spes*. Manuals and guides to understanding culture began to be published in the 1960s.[1]

A more recent outgrowth of the necessity of knowledge of culture for the preparation of missionaries has been interest in intercultural or cross-cultural communication. How cultural difference affects capacity to understand messages circulating in a given environment is now something many missionaries are encouraged to learn as part of their preparation for missionary work.

If indeed reconciliation is becoming a paradigm for mission, what will have to be included in the preparation of missionaries in the future? One would of course begin by noting that appropriate knowledge of relevant religious traditions in the locale in which the missionary will be working, as well as knowledge of the languages and cultures, will all continue to be important for the

1 Louis J. Luzbetak's *The Church and Cultures* (Techny, IL: Divine Word Publications, 1963) was among the first and most widely used. It is still in print forty years later, thanks to a Protestant publishing house, the William Carey Library.

missionary. It would be unimaginable that any of these could now fall by the wayside. However if we turn to reconciliation as the paradigm, there are some additional matters to be considered. Certainly first of all would be the theology and spirituality of reconciliation that were presented in the previous two lectures. An understanding of how God effects reconciliation in the world, and the missionary's role within activity would be foundational to any missionary activity. The differences and similarities between individual and social reconciliation would also need to be examined. The different dimensions of the work of reconciliation — as healing of memories, as reconstruction of societies after violence and conflict, as the creating safe and hospitable spaces in which the work of reconciliation might take place — all of these would require attention. Likewise, elements of the spirituality of reconciliation that inform the life and the work of the missionary would need to be inculcated in the new missionary: knowledge of one's own and others' wounds, the practice of contemplative prayer, creating safety and hospitality for victims all would have to be learned and practised. In other words, all of what has been discussed so far would need to find its way into the life and ethos of missionaries working within this paradigm.

At this point, I would want to take all the foregoing as something that could be presumed, and focus on a number of other areas. The theology and spirituality of reconciliation are still being developed and, one would hope, would continue to be developed in the years to come. In this presentation, I want to touch upon a number of areas that so far have not received as much attention, but will need to be examined more in the coming years. Some of these things have already been discovered in missionary work; others are known only in broad outline. Specifically, I want to explore here four areas: (1) the missionary and the experience of trauma in violent situations, (2) the missionary as mediating figure among different strata of the population, (3) the task of the missionary in pre-conflict, conflict, and post-conflict situations, and (4) processes of reconciliation in inter-religious situations. None of these can be examined in depth here; rather, the hope is to outline some of the issues for the preparation of missionaries which are raised in each of these areas and, in some instances, to give indications on what needs to be developed. My wish is to stimulate the kind of discussion necessary to give better shape to these issues of missionary formation.

The Missionary and the Experience of Trauma in Violent Situations

The very fact that reconciliation is even being discussed as a paradigm for mission implies a heightened level of violence and conflict in the world today. A brief outline of some of those factors — a reshaping of the world economic and political order, globalization, the emergence of new awareness of difference and ethnicity, multicultural societies - was sketched in the first presentation. It was the growing awareness of how overt conflict was affecting not just combatants in armies, but civilian populations themselves that prompted the new interest in reconciliation.

What about missionaries who enter environments of violence? What effect does it have upon them? We have quite a bit of experience with this already. Experiencing violence, either inflicted upon one's own person or witnessing it being done to others, can be traumatic. It entails a threat to one's sense of safety and well-being. When one lives for longer periods of time in situations of conflict, overt violence, or violent repression, it can have a long-term effect upon one's sense of self as well as one's relation to others.

The study of trauma and its effects has been developing for nearly a century. From the study of "shell shock" during the First World War, down to what is called in some psychiatric circles "Post-Traumatic Stress Disorder" (PTSD), a picture is emerging of how the experience of violence, either to oneself or witnessed to, can disorient a human being.

A frequent response to violence is to try to suppress the emotions which arise from it: fear, anger, insecurity, and the like. While this may not be a healthy response to violence, it may at times be the only means of survival, especially when one cannot escape the violence. Missionaries have a special vulnerability in all of this. Studies are showing that the stress of living in a new or previously unknown culture can lower the mechanisms of repression used to protect oneself. Thus, suppressed memories and emotions from an earlier stage of a missionary's life, such as childhood physical or sexual abuse, may come back to awareness because defence barriers are lowered. The self-image of the missionary as the hero-martyr[2] may delude the missionary into expecting invulnerability as the trademark of the good missionary. Or the missionary may be in the midst of such chaos and violence that his or her only concern is the rescue of others and not his or her own well-being. Closely related to this is what is sometimes called "survivor guilt," i.e., guilt that one has survived because of being a powerful foreigner while local people have perished.[3]

The consequences of not attending to the trauma that the missionary has experienced can be multiple: numbness, undue risk-taking, inappropriate behaviour, self-medication with alcohol or drugs, psychosomatic illness, sleeplessness, and other things. Because a paradigm of mission as reconciliation may lead to greater exposure of the missionary to violence, a number of steps need to be taken.

First of all, screening the missionary candidate's past should happen before the missionary leaves home for mission work. If there is evidence of childhood or later trauma, these events could have a negative effect on the missionary's self-image and performance. Sometimes the missionary calling itself can be trauma-induced: a way of fleeing one's memories and family, a way of proving to oneself and to God that one is acceptable even though defiled by abusive behaviour. Traumas of the past should at least be acknowledged, if not treated in some fashion, to alleviate their negative repercussions in the life of the missionary.

Second, missionaries should be equipped with a reasonable self-knowledge of how they respond to witnessing violence and conflict, if they do not have this already. They must have the ability to monitor their own responses to this, as well as how to detect unhealthy or inappropriate responses in their peers. How one deals with the consequences of violence and trauma is at least partially culturally conditioned in nature, although the most severe consequences have a somewhat predictable pattern. Knowing oneself, one's limits, and one's resources is an important part of

2 Angelyn Dries has explored this in "The Hero-Martyr Myth in the United States: Catholic International Foreign Missionary Literature, 1893-1925," *Missiology* 19 (1991) 305-314.

3 A good introduction to these and related issues can be found in Robert Grant, "Trauma in Missionary Life," *Missiology* 23 (1995) 71-83. In a wider sense, including but also going beyond missionary life, see his *The Way of the Wound: A Spirituality of Trauma and Transformation* (privately printed by the author).

equipping the missionary for work in reconciliation. From a spiritual perspective, this has already been touched upon in the previous presentation in the section on knowing one's wounds. That one has experienced trauma is not necessarily negative; if one has learned how to cope with it, the experience can be a resource in helping others. But not attending to the consequences of trauma at all has potentially damaging consequences not only to the missionary but also (if it educes risk-taking behaviour) can be damaging to others.

For those responsible for the supervision of missionaries in the field, it is important to secure resources to treat the effects of trauma and to sustain missionaries working in violent situations. Certainly among the best is the use of support groups among missionaries themselves which allows for self-monitoring and peer-care. "Reality checks" are also useful as well to see if people immersed in situations of conflict have maintained sound judgement in situations of danger.

The third area important in dealing with the effects of violence and trauma on missionaries is care for them when on furlough or when they return to their home countries. It was only about twenty-five years ago that "re-entry shock" came to be recognized as the correlate to initial "culture shock." Missionaries who have experienced trauma in the field may be returning home to family and peers who have no way of appreciating what the missionaries have experienced, or do not want to know. This can give missionaries a sense of isolation, even from their loved ones and their colleagues. Outlets must be found for them to examine and express what they have experienced. In some places organizations now exist where former missionaries can find sympathetic ears to listen to their stories.[4]

The experience of trauma and witnessing violence is something unfortunately all too common for missionaries today. Especially because of the commitment of so many missionaries to work with the poor and the marginalized, the chances that missionaries will find themselves in such circumstances is heightened. By devising reconciliation as a paradigm for mission, missionaries will, in some instances, be placed in situations of potential harm. It is

4 One such organization in the United States is FROM (Federation of Returned Overseas Missionaries), founded in 1976.

imperative, therefore, that as this paradigm develops, the care of missionaries in violent situations become a central concern.

The Social Position of the Missionary in the Reconciliation Paradigm

Missionaries, as expatriate religious leaders, occupy a special social position in schemes of reconciliation. They may indeed see themselves in total solidarity with the people they serve, and may be accepted as such by the people themselves. This has stood at the centre of the "option for the poor" which so many missionaries have exercised. Yet if they are expatriates they have to recognize a number of other features of their social position. They are likely better educated than many of the people they serve. If they maintain foreign citizenship or have an international missionary organization supporting them, they can be extricated from a difficult or dangerous social environment in a way that local people cannot. That may not affect their level of engagement with the people they serve, but it remains a social fact. Local people can acknowledge this and accept the missionaries' commitment to them as genuine. At the same time, local people know that the missionaries can leverage power in ways that their own leaders may not be able to do.

Likewise, being both within and outside of local communities, missionaries are able to access those higher in the social hierarchy than themselves. Conflict expert John Paul Lederach has characterized missionaries as being in the "hinge" position in conflict resolution, between the few public leaders at the top, and the many most affected by the conflict at the bottom.[5] He envisions the structure for the resolution of conflict as a pyramid. At the top of the pyramid are the few, highly visible national leaders, religious and political. These are the parties which forge peace agreements and sign treaties. While they may have access to the levers that start and stop conflicts, they are usually the most insulated from the direct effects of the conflict.

At the bottom is the "grass roots" population, the great masses of people. As civilians have become more and more implicated in conflicts, they are the most vulnerable to and least protected from

---

5 John Paul Lederach, *Building Peace: Sustainable Reconciliation in Divided Societies* (Washington: U.S. Institute of Peace, 1997), 39-61.

violence.[6] As civilian populations are becoming more used as pawns in the battle, pushed as displaced persons from one locale to another, terrorized by the competing sides, and stigmatized for the future (e.g., the use of the rape of women as military strategy), they are drawn more and more into the conflict whether they wish to choose to do so or not. In reconciliation processes, it is these great masses of people who need attention, as they become displaced or refugees, as they are subject to pressures they cannot avoid. In reconciliation processes after conflict, it is often the middle group, which includes regional leaders and expatriate missionaries, who occupy the mediating position. It is this "hinge" group who can make known the plight of the mass population to the leaders, and who can interpret back to the masses the treaties and agreements worked out by the elite. They likewise can warn the elite where the agreements they have reached will be viable on the ground below. They can also monitor whether agreements reached can continue to be effective or, if not, what conditions will have to be met for this to happen.

Because this kind of role is relatively new for many missionaries, it may require some change in self-perception on their part. Their total identification with the grassroots should not blind them to the fact that they may be in grassroots communities, but not entirely of those communities. This should not be perceived as negative; on the contrary they can be of genuine assistance to those communities in situations of negotiation and reconstruction. Preparing missionaries more consciously for this role may enhance their capacity to fulfil it when the situation arises.

Missionaries in the Three Stages of Conflict

A literature is appearing which examines potential roles for figures like missionaries in different stages of conflict.[7] This literature typically looks at three moments in the conflict situation: the pre-conflict stage, the conflict stage, and the post-conflict stage.

---

6 Part of this is due to the change in the nature of conflicts. In World War I, only about 11% of the civil population was directly affected by combat. At the end of the twentieth century, in the conflict in Kosovo, the number had jumped to 96%.

7 See for example *Working for Reconciliation: A Caritas Manual* (Vatican City: Caritas Internationalis, 1999); Joseph G. Bock, *Sharpening Conflict Management: Religious Leadership and the Double-Edged Sword* (Westport, CT: Praeger, 2001); Cjeka and Bamat, op. cit.; Joseph G. Bock and Clark McCauley, "A Call to Lateral Mission: Mobilizing Religious Authority against Ethnic Violence," *Mission Studies* 39 (2003), forthcoming.

In the pre-conflict stage, the missionary is involved in *conflict prevention*. This entails missionaries using their religious authority to keep "conflict producing" agents at bay. The credibility of the missionaries with their own religious group—and as far as that might extend for other religious groups—is what such conflict prevention turns upon. Among the activities in this pre-conflict are *rumour control*, that is, preventing incendiary rumours to spread about the purported activities of the other group; *stopping broad attributions* of the potential actions of a firebrand few to the intentions of the entire group; *reality checking*, that is, trying to ascertain if news that circulates corresponds to reality; *setting up communication networks*, so that information communicated can circulate quickly and effectively; *countering stereotypes* that impugn the other group; *maintain contact* with the leadership of the counterpart group; and *curb excessive rhetoric* that will cause situations to deteriorate. Likewise, effective religious leaders in pre-conflict situations work with their membership to create multiple modes of identification by belonging to different groups. This helps cut down the easy divide into "us and them." Sometimes, outside agitators will act so as to disrupt what had been relatively peaceable relations between groups at the local level. All of the skills just mentioned regarding communication, plus reminding local people of attitudes of trust and authority can serve to counter these destructive moves at least to some extent. At times, conflict cannot be avoided, particularly if relations have been deteriorating over a longer period of time, or long-standing grievances have not been addressed. When that happens, missionaries will find themselves in the second stage, conflict itself.

Cjeka and Bamat[8] found in their study of seven cases of action by grassroots religious leaders that, when full-scale conflict has broken out, efforts to quell the conflict by religious leaders is generally fruitless. What religious leaders resort to in the face of all-out conflict is rescue efforts aimed at protecting the most vulnerable during the conflict. This involves ensuring as best one can the safety of children, women, and the elderly; prevention of widespread physical destruction if possible; and ensuring accuracy

8 Cjeka and Bamat, op. cit.; Joseph G. Bock and Clark McCauley, "A Call to Lateral Mission: Mobilizing Religious Authority against Ethnic Violence," *Mission Studies* 39 (2003), forthcoming.

of communication, both at the grassroots level and to elites in a position to stop the conflict. This may seem to be meagre in the face of violence, but it is frequently all that is realistically possible when conflict has turned to overt violence. Truth is often the first casualty of war, it has been said. Chronicling the truth as best as one has access to it may serve future, post-conflict situations the best. Ensuring safety for the vulnerable also has to be a priority.

The role of the missionary in the post-conflict situation has been covered generally in the first presentation. Working in whatever way possible to re-establish truth-telling, to initiate justice, and to ensure the rule of law are the foundational works to be undertaken. The missionary must help set up networks of collaboration to make venues for the healing of memories possible; an area already addressed at some length. One point should be added here. Not infrequently the fault lines of division in a society run right down the centre of the Church. What then needs to be done is truth-telling within the Church, so that the Church, as much as possible, can serve as a model for what the rest of society might hope to become. Doing less than that will cost the Church credibility and a role in the reconciliation process.

And most importantly, the missionary must work toward aiding the moral reconstruction of society. That is done especially by attending to the symbolic dimensions and implications of decisions taken. Do the decisions represent the kind of society we wish to become? Will they lead us along a path that corresponds to our best lights? Hasty manufacturing of decisions can short-circuit the long-term hopes for the future.

What does all of this mean for the preparation of missionaries? It means first of all that missionaries have to be aware of the social dynamics of each of the stages of conflict. Key to their being able to act is understanding the possibilities and the limitations of their roles as leaders and as what are termed "insider outsiders." It is their moral authority, which will enable them to do whatever can be done. Certain aspects of the roles mentioned in each of the three stages can be learned. Other parts of them simply must be intuited when the time comes. Because every conflict is different in its origins and the manner in which it builds up and explodes, so too the resolution of conflict and the type of reconciliation needed afterward will never be quite the same.

Reconciliation in Interreligious Settings

The work of reconciliation frequently has to be carried out in interreligious settings, i.e., where adherents to more than one religious tradition are present. The vision of reconciliation presented here has been one deeply informed by Christian faith. It is important to note at the outset here that reconciliation is viewed differently in other religious traditions.[9] In Judaism, more attention is given to the conversion of the wrongdoer than to the role of victim. In Islam, more emphasis is given on the role of the mediation of the dispute than either of the contending parties. Buddhism emphasizes the role of self-awareness within the situation.

This might be a convenient time to emphasize once again the role of culture in reconciliation processes. Many cultures, especially small-scale cultures where the co-operation of all is needed to survive, have rituals of reconciliation to which all agree to adhere. The ritual element is important here, since engaging in such patterned behaviour underscores the fact that what is happening is larger than any single individual involved in the conflict. Many cultures celebrate the moment of reconciliation itself with a communal meal, where once contending parties now eat together. In any situation of conflict, it is important to know just what cultural resources are available to help effect reconciliation.

Interreligious situations pose two different scenarios for reconciliation and peacemaking. In the first scenario religious difference has been part of the conflict itself, and so dealing with religious difference becomes essential if there is to be reconciliation. Religious difference, if you will, is part of the problem. In the second scenario, religious difference has not been the principal reason for the conflict; other factors can be identified. In this situation, if you will, religion can be a resource for reconciliation and part of the solution.

---

9 For a brief overview of the different traditions, see *Peacebuilding*, op. cit., 29-32. For more on Judaism, see Marc Gopin, "Forgiveness as an element of conflict resolution in religious cultures: Walking the tightrope of reconciliation and justice," in Mohammed Abu-Nimer, *Reconciliation, Coexistence, and Justice in Interethnic Conflict* (New York: Lexington Books, 2001); on Islam, Mohammed Abu-Nimer, *Nonviolence and Peacebuilding in Islam* (Gainsville, FL: University of Florida Press, 2003); on Buddhism, Thich Nhat Thanh, *Being Peace* (Berkeley: Parallax Books, 1987).

It should be noted at the outset that all the great religious traditions view themselves as religions of peace. They can point to central elements in their traditions that make peace an essential part of experience of the transcendent and a key component in human well-being. At the same time, there are identifiable parts of each of their histories, and sometimes instances in their sacred texts that appear to condone or even justify violence. Adherents of the respective traditions are often quick to downplay this history and those texts in their own tradition, but sometimes are equally quick to note instances of violence in the traditions of others.

In situations where religion has been called upon to support violent behaviour, one must always first begin by ascertaining whether it was the religious tradition that initiated the violence, or whether it was used as a convenient foil to cover other motives, such as greed, the will to power, or group solidarity. Because all the great traditions make some sort of absolute claim, wrapping one's motives in the mantle of religion can produce an instant legitimacy for certain kinds of behaviour. An example would be the cultivation of "hindutva" by Indian fundamentalists. The ostensive reason is that India is for Hindus only. A more likely reason is that low-caste Hindus are converting to Christianity, Islam, and Buddhism because they are receiving better treatment than they do from high-caste Hindus. This is eroding the Hindu political base. By making a neat identification of religion with the group's interests, no further justification need be sought. Engaging in violence becomes the will of God. This is especially the case where the lines of ethnicity and religious adherence coincide. It is an utterly convenient way to spur people into action.

How does one seek reconciliation in these settings? One has to begin by gauging the power relations between the two groups. If those relations are too lopsided (e.g., a Christian minority over against a Muslim majority, or a Muslim minority over against a Hindu majority), then there is little space to manoeuvre, especially if one is in the minority position. If there is room for movement, one needs to begin a process whereby multiple identification is possible; that is to say, that groups with which one can identify do not coincide exactly with religious adherence. This has been effective in places such as Northern Ireland, where Catholic and Protestant children belong to the same group and intermingle. A second strategy is to expose generalizations about the other. When the other is defined as individuals with distinctive personalities rather than a common stereotype, then there is the possibility for breaking down barriers of separation.[10] Put simply, the playing field has to move from a dichotomy of us-versus-them to a more complex picture, where stereotypes and assumptions are challenged. Many of the strategies discussed about under conflict prevention are appropriate here.

Third, if there is a longer history of coexistence, then that history must be recalled, and the question raised why there is conflict now. If there had been a peaceful coexistence earlier, then perhaps the stimulus to conflict is coming from outside. Knowing this can allow a divided community to close ranks against outside agitation. If one of the religious parties is a recent arrival, due to government resettlement policies or refugee status, then that feature should become part of public awareness, since it shifts the onus of the conflict from religious belonging to other sources.

In the second scenario, where religion can be a resource and part of the solution to the conflict, a number of principles and strategies are in play. The first principle is respecting the role religion can play in the situation. For missionaries coming from secularized countries, the tendency is to invoke a secularism that marginalizes or privatizes the place of religion in the situation. This grows out of the missionaries' experience in their home country. But in many of the places where missionaries come to work, religion is a very public phenomenon and of utmost importance in the lives of people. So instead of trying to create a secular playing field for the resolution of conflict, one has to create one of religious pluralism. That involves not only mutual respect among the religious traditions present, but also an ever-increasing knowledge of traditions other than one's own. Religion cannot be pushed to the sidelines in these situations, but must be acknowledged as an important feature.

Second, those mediating the conflict must insure that there is equal opportunity and equal access for the traditions. That is to say, one tradition must not gain privilege over the others. If there are prayers as part of the process, then all traditions should be represented. If financial resources are available, then decisions about how these might be used should be taken collectively. To do

10 I deal with seven of the most common generalizations in *Reconciliation: Mission and Ministry in a Changing Social Order* (Maryknoll, NY: Orbis, 1992), 52f.

so is a way of implementing some of the principles presented earlier. To provide equal opportunity is a sign of respect for the religious traditions, and therefore also of their adherents. Showing respect helps build trust and create the safe space in which further negotiation can happen. Equal access promotes a sense of belonging and participation, creating the hospitable environment that will allow the parties to work together in the future. If people feel things are being done to them or for them, that will lessen the investment those parties have in the process.

Third, those mediating the situation must work as much as possible with the resources of each of the traditions rather than around them. This entails an increasing knowledge of the tradition of the other. Again, this helps to complexify the picture in a healthy way, avoiding the resort to stereotypes and other generalizations.

Respect, tolerance, inclusion, participation, and a greater knowledge of the traditions of others are attitudes and skills that can be learned. And what has been learned can be sustained and deepened by a spirituality of reconciliation. In the preparation of missionaries to be agents of reconciliation, thinking about and interacting with these scenarios can enhance missionaries' capacity to operate effectively in an interreligious environment.

Conclusion

In looking at different dimensions of the preparation of the missionary to work in a paradigm of reconciliation as mission, I hope that it has become evident that what might be done by way of preparation is not simply a response to challenges arising from the environment. The different mediating roles the missionary can play flow also out of the theology of reconciliation. The care of the missionary in the face of trauma fits closely with the spirituality of reconciliation in its elements of self-knowledge, the situation of the role of the agent of reconciliation within God's work, and acknowledgement of the limits of what we as God's agents can do.

Will reconciliation as a paradigm of mission fade away if the world becomes a less contentious place? The latter is unlikely, given the forces of globalization and the increasing pluralism in so many places in the world today. But even were that to happen, my intuition is that this paradigm will not disappear anytime soon.

That is because it represents a rediscovery of a fundamental theological understanding of God's work in the world. It helps us see the form the *missio dei* is taking for us. To be sure, as the world continues to change, other issues make take on greater urgency. For example, further ecological deterioration, or the scarcity of drinking water in some parts of the world may become issues which must be addressed immediately. But how God is reconciling the world is something that is likely to stay with us for a long, long time. As a form of mission, the experience of reconciliation can give us one of the most direct and intense experiences of the divine in our lives. And that experience of God-among-us is something which we will always treasure.

Part II

RECONCILIATION BEYOND CONFLICT

FROM VIOLENCE TO PEACE: REFLECTIONS FROM NORTHERN IRELAND

Cecelia Clegg

Introduction

Serious inter-community violence or the threat of violence is a reality in Northern Ireland even though we are eight years into a post-cease-fire peace process. When I left home for the airport en route to this conference, my taxi had to wend its way past a long line of heavily armoured army and police vehicles and through groups of heavily clad riot police and soldiers. North Belfast was geared up once again for the Orange Order's 'Tour of the North' parade. The security forces were once again the buffer between the Catholic area of Ardoyne, in which I live, and a group of Protestant marchers. The scene is depressingly familiar.

In this short paper, I am going to look first at the nature of the violence we face and its relationship to religion. Then I will sketch out some of the roles, both positive and negative, that the churches and faith communities have played especially in the last thirty years. Finally, I will outline some key theological tasks which face Christian communities in the post-cease-fire reconstruction of Northern Irish society. I am using the phrase 'churches and faith communities' in order to include the many smaller Christian groups who do not recognise themselves as churches but who play a significant role on the island of Ireland. Of necessity, therefore, I will be able only to touch briefly upon some major themes, like sectarianism, which in their own right could command the focus of an entire conference.

1. Violence and Religion

I have quite deliberately chosen to describe the Ardoyne and the marchers by their religious labels rather than their political ones, Nationalist/Republican or Unionist/Loyalist, in order to highlight the malign mix of religion and politics which is at the heart of the conflict in Northern Ireland. The violence that we have to overcome is an antagonised religious-political division which is usually referred to as sectarianism, and is alive and well despite the ongoing peace process. Indeed, there is a case to be made that the level of sectarian tension on the streets is actually higher now than pre-ceasefire, and there are compelling reasons why this might be so. I want to be clear that when I use the word 'sectarianism' I do not use it with the sociology of religions definition which distinguishes 'churches' and 'sects,' nor do I mean simply 'religious hatred.' Rather, I am referring to the systemic phenomenon which we find in these islands and elsewhere, which my colleague, Joseph Liechty and I, have defined in our book *Moving Beyond Sectarianism* as:

A system of attitudes, actions, beliefs, and structures

: at personal, communal and institutional levels

: which always involve religion and usually involve a negative mixing of religion and politics.

: which arises as a distorted expression of positive human needs, especially for belonging, identity and the free expression of difference and is expressed in destructive patterns of relating

: hardening the boundaries between groups: overlooking others

: belittling, dehumanising, or demonising others

: justifying or collaborating in the domination of others

: physically intimidating or attacking others[1]

---

1 This definition is taken from Joseph Liechty and Cecelia Clegg, *Moving Beyond Sectarianism: Religion, Conflict and Reconciliation in Northern Ireland* (Dublin: Columba Press, 2001), pp. 102-3.

I make the distinction because I am conscious that in at least some of the current debate about sectarianism in Scotland the word is used variously in its sociological definition,[2] or to mean primarily 'religious hatred.'[3]

In Northern Ireland groups of Catholic and Protestant Christians have developed their identities in opposition to, or negatively over against, one another in such a way that they need a threatening other to keep a stable sense of their own identity.[4] Hence the massive upheaval caused by the peace process. As one Belfast person dryly observed: "we knew who we were when we were fighting one another, but who are we now?" Moreover, these communal identities are, as the late political scientist Frank Wright observed, inextricably both religious and national.[5] So by and large, Catholic also indicates Irish and Republican or Nationalist, Protestant indicates British and Loyalist or Unionist, though there are, of course, exceptions. This religious - national identification persists even where religious practice has ceased and the religious label has become a relatively contentless boundary marker.

There have been attempts to break out of this oppositional situation, politically for example, the formation of the Women's Coalition, a small political party comprised consciously of people from both of the larger traditions; and religiously through the local inter-church groups which try to live in honest communion with one another.

It is important, in order to understand what the churches and faith communities have being struggling with in Northern Ireland, to realise how pervasive the sectarian system actually is. For many

---

2 See the comments of Ian Wilson, Grand Master of the Orange Lodge of Scotland where he argues: "As far as I know, the Kirk is full of Presbyterians which makes us sectarian." in Lynne Robertson, "Sectarianism in Scotland: Shame of the Past or Stain on the Future," *Life and Work: The Editorially Independent Magazine of the Church of Scotland* (January 2003), p.9

3 For example, its use by the Scottish executive Cross-Party Working Group on Religious Hatred in its report: *Tackling Religious Hatred* (www.scotland.gov.uk, 13 March 2003)

4 See Marc Gopin, "The Heart of the Stranger," (unpublished paper, Boundaries and Bonds Conference, Stranmillis College, Belfast, June, 1997) and Alan Falconer, "Remembering" in *Reconciling Memories,* rev. ed., eds Alan Falconer and Joseph Liechty (Blackrock, Co Dublin: Columba Press, 1998), p.13.

5 Frank Wright, "Reconciling the Histories: Protestant and Catholic in Northern Ireland," in *Reconciling Memories,* rev. ed., eds Falconer and Liechty, p.34.

people and communities, the sectarian system has determined and still determines where they may live, where they may work, where they may shop, to whom they may sell land, where they may be educated, with whom they may marry and with whom they may socialise. This system has been developing over centuries and it is now so efficient that it no longer requires acts of violence to regenerate itself; it can in fact take ordinary people's reasonable fears and even the best pastoral efforts of ministers and turn them into ways to further underline the divide. For example, the reasonable fear of attack felt by those living as a religious- national minority in a housing development often leads them to seek segregated housing 'among their own.' This reinforces the divide. In terms of pastoral ministry, the current model in most churches, tacitly or explicitly, regards ministers as appointed primarily to work among their own, with their own and on behalf of their own, reaching out to others only as necessary and in some cases only to proselytise them. If ministry is lived without sufficient regard for and meaningful contact with other traditions it similarly risks underlining the divisions.

I am deliberately choosing ordinary, apparently non-violent examples to try to show how sectarianism can be perpetuated and reinforced by good, educated, well-intentioned Christians, who sit in our places of worship, and serve on our committees, and who individually do not have a sectarian bone in their bodies. The gross expressions in rioting, bomb attacks, shootings and beatings are only one facet of an extremely complex and resistant phenomenon which both faces and enmeshes the churches and faith communities in Northern Ireland.

In truth, there is no innocent place to stand in our society because the systemic nature of sectarianism means that all are implicated, if only by omission. The ministry of reconciliation in these circumstances is both difficult and perilous.

2. The Role of the Churches and Faith Communities during the Troubles

As an outsider to Northern Ireland I am in no doubt that the violence and destruction in society could have been imaginably worse if it had not been for the moderating influence of the churches and faith communities. Yes, they were and are part of the problem; and certainly there were voices from within the Christian community who can be construed as having exacerbated the situation at times, but even this agitation was not the whole of what those particular voices had to contribute.[6] Churches as institutions, faith communities, and individual ministers, often acted prophetically and with courage. They shouldered well the burden of day by day, week by week preaching the gospel of non-violence, forgiveness, repentance, and no retaliation; of visiting the victims, burying the dead, consoling the bereaved, counselling the perpetrators, striving for justice, and advising politicians who were seeking to find a political way forward. Individual Christians too, like Gordon Wilson and Michael McGoldrick, stayed the hand of retaliation by paramilitaries of their own tradition through their passionate, grief-stricken appeals in the wake of their losses.

Even at the institutional level churches, particularly the four larger churches: Methodist, Presbyterian, Catholic and Church of Ireland, began to move towards co-operating more closely. A regular meeting of the leaders of these four was put in place so that there was increased communication between them and opportunities to act together, if that seemed appropriate. This was a courageous step forward which works more or less well depending on who holds the leadership posts at any given time. Religious communities, in particular some Catholic religious houses like Clonard Redemptorist Monastery in the heart of Republican West Belfast, created safe spaces for Republican politicians and paramilitary leaders to come together to talk and to develop trust and understanding with their Loyalist and Protestant counterparts. Little is known of the secret history of the Troubles period, or of the countless people who worked quietly in the background, at times risking their own safety to be involved in conversations or to carry messages between parties. If it is ever published I suspect it will make fascinating but sobering reading.

There is, however, another side to the role played by churches and faith communities, as it were a shadow side, which is very much influenced by and, it must be said, helps to sustain the sectarian ethos of society. Churches and faith communities rather

---

6 See the report of a heated exchange between Iris Robinson and ex-prisoners, who had served time for fighting Republicans, in which they accuse her, her husband (DUP deputy leader Peter Robinson) and DUP leader Ian Paisley of "encouraging others to do it." *Beyond Fife and Drum: Report of* a *Conference held on Belfast's Shankill Road, October* 1994, Island pamphlets, no.11 (Newtownabbey, Northern Ireland: Island Publications, 1995), pp. 35-6.

than seeking to reconcile the oppositional relationships between the traditions and seeking to model a different form of relating, have become thoroughly caught, up in those negative dynamics. They reflect rather than challenge the behaviour of society. They are guilty of what Croatian theologian Miroslav Volf, reflecting about the tragedy in Rwanda, describes as an 'idolatrous shift in loyalty.'[7] In other words, they have allowed loyalty to their nation or to the movement of nationalism to become their ultimate allegiance and to taint, distort and in some cases to subvert the being and mission of church. Northern Irish priests, ministers, and pastors, even those most active in urging politicians to find a peaceful settlement, failed and still fail to grasp that in a situation of antagonised religious - political division, religious organisations as well as political parties need to take proactive steps to establish at least ongoing dialogue, if not fully co-operative relationship between them. Dialogue is crucial not for its own sake but to help their constituencies grow in the type of respect for one another that can ultimately sustain peace.

This idolatrous shift of loyalty, a classic temptation for Christians in any situation of hot and protracted civil war, was particularly so in Northern Ireland. It is well known that the dynamics of conflict tend to draw groups more tightly together around a leader and set of ideals, and often have the force to hold people, even when they disagree with the leader or the ideals. Nation and nationalism have a particularly strong appeal and this was reinforced by the fact that Protestant and Catholic traditions on the island of Ireland historically are aligned closely with different national identities. Moreover, since safety is found in belonging to one or other camp, people do not even publicly criticise their own, whatever they might say among themselves, because criticism is equated with weakening their 'side.' The life of the few who have tried to stand between the two traditions has been, and is, both lonely and dangerous.

The development of religious-national identity has been exacerbated by a number of other factors: self-absorption, fear, theological convictions, and disdain. Our research during the

---

7 Miroslav Volf, "The Social meaning of Reconciliation," *Interpretation,* vol 54, no 2, (April 2000), p. 159.

Moving Beyond Sectarianism project suggests that many churches and faith communities are quite simply self- absorbed. They find life within their own community or group so interesting and fulfilling that they have neither the time nor the inclination to reach beyond their boundaries, especially when such outreach will involve difficult and uneasy conversation and relationship.

Fear too plays a part in inhibiting outreach, though this is more true for Protestants than for Catholics. Christian community leaders and members fear hostile reactions from their own congregations, parishes, societies or groups if they act in friendship or openness towards the 'other'. One Presbyterian minister, who showed solidarity by standing with Catholic colleagues during a particularly ugly series of incidents some years ago outside the Catholic church in Harryville, County Antrim, remarked that it was the "good suits" in his congregation with whom he had most difficult afterwards. Internal pressure within Christian groups means that that the cost of crossing the boundaries that divide can be high.

Theological convictions exacerbate the tendency to relationships of religious- national opposition in a particularly corrosive way. There are numerous convictions, which can prove problematic, and I have not the scope to address them all here. I will select two, one Protestant and one Catholic, which I regard as among the most urgently in need of attention and action today, namely anti-Catholicism and self-sufficiency.

I would defend the right of people to make truth claims and to disagree with the beliefs and practices of any group. The manner in which those claims are made or refuted, however, is crucial for the development of respect and ongoing relationship. The attitude of anti-Catholicism prevalent in many Protestant groupings, including the larger denominations, is problematic because the way in which it is expressed often leads at least to the hardening of boundaries between the traditions, sometimes to belittling or demonising Catholics, and in more extreme forms could be taken as justifying attempted domination. Some of the anti-Catholic sentiment is based on misunderstandings of Catholic beliefs and practices; some is born of fear and hatred. It is of deep concern that Protestant denominations have done so little to challenge destructive and factually inaccurate anti-Catholicism when it is expressed within their congregations and assemblies. It is equally problematic that the Catholic Church as an institution does not challenge these attitudes publicly, expressing the wounds that such attitudes inflict and offering an accurate account of Catholic faith. Churches and faith communities are still too reticent to let the other know how offensive or destructive the other's behaviour or pronouncements are - this too is a legacy of violent conflict. There is a famous saying in Northern Ireland taken from a poem by Seamus Heaney: "Whatever you say, say nothing." How well we live that dictum and often to the detriment of honest relationships.

The Catholic church, despite the changes brought about during the second Vatican Council, still shows limited openness to other Christian churches, regarding them variously as 'ecclesial communities' or 'true particular churches,' but holding that all suffer from defects.[8] The belief that the "unique church of Christ ...subsists in the Catholic Church," reiterated in the document, *Dominus Jesus,* which was published in the year 2000, leads, I believe, to an attitude of self-sufficiency which militates against productive inter-church relationships. In Northern Ireland, Catholics tend to be willing to take part in inter-church events, but these rank low on the list of priorities in parish life. They are, as it were, an optional extra for those who are interested in them, but are seen as largely peripheral to the process of peacemaking, which is regarded as a mainly political process. This self-sufficient mode of being, is difficult to challenge because it is not 'anti' Protestantism, it is not aggressive or overtly offensive, it seems simply indifferent. It does, however, make it very difficult for Protestant churches, faith communities, and groups to find ways to connect with or to access Catholic structures in order to open up meaningful dialogue or co-operation. For example, until this month, with the setting up of the Catholic Commission on Social Affairs, the Catholic Church in Ireland had no structure which corresponded to the Church and Government committee of the Presbyterian Church, the Board of Social Responsibility of the Methodist Church, and the Church and Society Committee of the Church of Ireland. The new commission only operates in the five Northern dioceses, but it provides a much needed channel of connection giving the four larger churches the possibility of

---

8 Declaration *Dominus Jesus: on the Unicity and Salvific Universality of Jesus Christ and the Church* (Rome: Congregation for the Doctrine of the Faith, September 2000), paragraph 17.

working at official, rather than ad hoc, level on societal issues in the North.

The last factor that I want to address, which augments the divisive effect of the religious - national identity of churches, is disdain. Disdain is an intentional dynamic in which people choose to keep themselves separate from others because they dislike, disagree with, scorn or despise what they say, do, or stand for. It is usually not a reasoned stance and is largely fed by myth, rumour, and ignorance of the other. One of its more destructive aspects is that the scornful separation engendered means that people stop listening to what the other has to say. They are thereby cut off from any reasonable chance to understand the other's position or to have their myths about them debunked. Lurking behind the dynamic of disdain is a thinly veiled sense of superiority.

What I am arguing, then, is that churches and faith communities have significantly held back the tide of violence and have ministered faithfully to their flocks. They have even created some safe spaces where political groups were able to forge elements of the eventual political agreement. But through it all, churches and faith communities have, until very recently, signally failed to take responsibility for their own contribution to the antagonised division.[9] Nor have they been able to look honestly and together at their resources for helping to build a sustainable peace. The predominant theology of mission that I discern in this period has been one of 'proclamation' either by the Word in Protestant traditions or by being and ritual in the Catholic tradition.

3. Rebuilding Society

Northern Ireland is, I believe, experiencing a critical moment of history. The political peace process has brought us a certain distance towards overcoming the violence and division, and it has seriously faltered. A lack of basic trust between parties is more than the fragile political relationships can bear. Politicians who have been courageously driving the peace process forward now

---

9 After the report to General Synod by the Working Party on Sectarianism in 1999 the Church of Ireland has been designing a process to involve the denomination island-wide in a reflection on 'Sectarianism and Dealing with Difference.' The process began in 2001 with a survey of attitudes to difference which will form the basis of an educational programme. The results of the survey were published after General Synod, May 2003, Gareth I. Higgins, *The Hard Gospel: dealing positively with the difference in Northern Ireland* (Dublin, Church of Ireland, May 2003).

need urgent and focussed support from the rest of civic society. They need more than the encouragement and cheerleading from the sidelines which got them through the negotiations that gave us the Belfast Agreement in 1998. The moral reconstruction of Northern Ireland requires that all organisations and citizens attend to and participate in the conversations and steps which will re-imagine the society. This critical moment is one in which Northern Ireland is faced with the choice to put down its divisions and oppositional identities once and for all, and to will a peaceful co-existence of all its communities and traditions or to remain in a stasis which is likely, eventually, to slide towards renewed violence. The transition to peaceful co- existence will not happen overnight. Politicians alone cannot deliver the reconstruction, nor can the churches and faith communities.

Christian institutions, nonetheless, have a very significant role to play because they still hold widespread influence. To be effective, however, they are going to need to let their theology of mission as proclamation move into the background and embrace a theology of mission as dialogue. Their participation in the moral reconstruction of Northern Ireland requires, at the very least, that they begin institutionally to cross boundaries to talk with and to listen to those of other traditions. I envisage that this dialogue will develop at least three axes: from blame to responsibility; from opposition to forbearance; and from separation to positive engagement.

The movement from blame to responsibility is primary; it is the activity of truth telling. Churches and faith communities will firstly have to admit the truth about their part in the conflict in their own assemblies and then tell it publicly. They will also learn to be communities of truth listening, ready to receive stories and to help speakers to articulate all that needs to be said no matter how painful. The key theological task of this movement is repentance.

The movement from opposition to forbearance will be a lengthy process of finding ways to help to heal wounds. Churches and faith communities will identify and acknowledge their own wounds, not as a badge of victimhood, but in order to be better able both to recognise and to empathise with the wounds of others. This process will also call forth the symbolic creativity of Christian practice and ritual. The key theological task of this axis will be forgiveness.

The axis, separation to positive engagement, will be a progressively building phase as communities share the truth, grieve together, repent, ask and receive forgiveness, and start to envisage a new future together. This will be the most difficult and potentially the most effective aspect of the dialogue, because it promises a modelling of newness of relationship. This newness will be present in relationships within each tradition as well as in the cross - tradition sphere. The key theological task of this process is *kenosis,* self-emptying; allowing God to radically reshape identities in conformity to Christ. This will mean a painful pruning away or hollowing out the parts of our communal identities that do not serve God's mission of reconciliation, of bringing everything into life-giving relationship.

Conclusion

The part played by churches and faith communities in the conflict has been, like the curate's egg, good in parts. Despite increasing secularisation and the natural tendency in the post-conflict period, for people to scapegoat religious institutions, Christian communities have a crucial role to play in the reconstruction of society. Their ability to do so will, I believe, depend on their capacity to live dialogue, repentance, forgiveness, and self-emptying.

BEARING WITNESS TO THE OVERCOMER OF VIOLENCE

Reflections from a practitioner theologian in Northern Ireland

David Porter

At the end of her book, *Wifework*,[1] Susan Maushart recalls the scene in John Steinbeck's epic novel, *The Grapes of Wrath*, where an official is sent to repossess the land of a farmer. As the farmer responds out of his anxiety and distress the official complains 'Don't go blaming me, all I know is I've got my orders.' 'Who are your orders from?' asks the farmer. 'Nobody, it's a company' replies the official. The farmer probes further 'Does the company have a president?' 'Don't go blaming him' says the official, 'the bank tells him what to do.' And so the dialogue continues until in exasperation the farmer cries – 'Well, who do I shoot then!'

For Steinbeck, the fact that there is no clear culprit is an essential part of the tragedy. Speaking of the crisis facing marriage but I think applicable to our situation in Northern Ireland, Maushart comments:

> "Nobody and nothing is to blame; and yet responsibility for the crisis belongs to all of us. First order of business is to recognise our complicity, without beating ourselves up or anybody else up either. …the challenge is to understand our past behaviour and to take responsibility for producing change for the future."[2]

Beyond the Blame Game

In their book *Moving Beyond Sectarianism*, Cecelia Clegg and Joe Liechty quote feminist theologian, Fran Porter, who warns that the systemic nature of sectarianism while of necessity involving everyone, must be presented as such without 'apportioning

1 Susan Maushart, *Wifework : what marriage really means for women.* (Bloomsbury 2002)

2 Maushart p.246

paralysing chunks of blame.'[3] Liechty and Clegg go on to comment:

> "Given that sectarianism builds and relies on a culture of blame, our response has been to find ways of promoting a culture of responsibility."[4]

In bearing witness to the overcomer of violence those involved in the calling and ministry of reconciliation have to consider how to move the Christian faith community (and indeed wider society) beyond the blame game. For any critique of the church, whether in relation to the identity conflict in Ireland, the cover up of clerical abuse or the subordination of women, must, if it is to be constructive, elicit responsibility for the cause while nurturing a capacity for change.

ECONI[5] came in to being to challenge Evangelical Protestants, on the basis of biblical values, concerning their failure to bear witness to the peaceable kingdom. Our concern was to nurture a spirit of repentance for both the idolatry of a politicised faith represented by the slogan 'For God and Ulster' and the pietistic escape from responsibility that had marked Evangelical responses to the conflict. The danger was, and always remains, that instead of creating the necessary change of attitude and actions, we contribute to the paralysing of the Evangelical Protestant community by an uncritical absorption of caricature and false guilt.

When faced with deep-rooted, historic identity conflicts all Christian leaders need to recognise this danger in seeking change in their community. We can unthinkingly participate in the general paralysis of the church under the scathing critique of secular humanism, which, while rightly challenging the contribution of religion to conflict, retains a vested interest in beating up the church to marginalise its contribution to the future peace. In Northern Ireland it is easy to blame bad religion. While the ministry of reconciliation may indeed call us to function as

---

3 Joseph Liechty and Cecelia Clegg, *Moving Beyond Sectarianism: Religion, Conflict and Reconciliation in Northern Ireland* (Columba Press 2001) p.17

4 Liechty and Clegg p.18

5 Evangelical Contribution On Northern Ireland emerged in 1987 as a mainstream Evangelical response to the community conflict, with the primary aim of addressing fellow Evangelicals on their biblical responsibility to make peace and to reflect the kingdom values that require a questioning of cultural and political loyalties. For more information the website is found at www.econi.org.

scapegoat in our service of the world,[6] leaders need to take a realistic account of this dynamic of false blame as the church takes its place in the public space of the future.

There is vigorous debate concerning the role of religion in the Irish conflict. While rejecting those who would dismiss its significance it is nevertheless necessary to warn against an oversimplification of the conflict as being religious. It is now widely accepted that while there is a religious dimension to the conflict and even a significant religious contribution to its source and nurture, the conflict in Ireland is not essentially and fundamentally a conflict about religion. While not absolving the churches of their responsibility it does require that we stop beating ourselves up or allowing ourselves to be beat up for our apparent failure to stop the conflict.

This perspective comes out of deep frustration. The community from which I come is perceived as the historic oppressor. Yet over the course of 'the troubles'[7] many Protestant church leaders have been at the forefront of calling the church and wider society to repentance and reconciliation. Giving leadership and voice to such challenge and change is to be located in a fragile place. To then find that colleagues in the church both inside and outside of Northern Ireland still want to beat you up on the basis of an ill informed understanding of the complexity of the context brings it own emotional vulnerability.

Ironically it may be that because we fear finding ourselves on the margins of a secular future, we keep colluding in our own complicity by talking up the religious factor of the conflict in the forlorn hope of securing a redeeming role in putting it right. So while accepting the need for the church to take responsibility for its complicity and exhibit a true repentance of actions that build the peace, it is time for the beating to stop. I want to reflect on the witness of the church in a constructive manner that moves us beyond the blame game.

---

6 Leviticus 16:20-22 There is a profoundly biblical ministry for the people of God in any society to embrace the vocation of scapegoat. The image of 'bearing the sin' of the community before God and with it being driven into the wilderness for the sake of atonement and reconciliation is worthy of further reflection for the church when looking for metaphors to understand its role in certain contexts.

7 The current phase of the historic conflict lasting 30 years from the civil disturbance in 1968 to the Belfast Agreement of 1998 is in Northern Ireland commonly referred to as 'the troubles'.

This we will do under three headings. First to make some comments about the context in Northern Ireland, as I understand it, essentially setting out some of the presuppositions I hold in our ongoing process. Then I want to reflect on aspects of the church's role over the last thirty years. Finally I will bring some of the learning from our setting to the theme of reconciliation.

Context

There are three presuppositions I currently hold that help set the context for the reconciling mission of the church in Northern Ireland.

Post-Troubles but not Post-Conflict

We live in a community that is post-troubles but not post-conflict. Fifteen years in the peacemaking task leads me to believe that our conflict is here to stay for a very long time. It is unlikely in my lifetime nor for at least another two generations that we will genuinely reimagine our relationships beyond the defining dynamics that have been the root cause of our conflict. The western liberal idea proposes that if you put people together in a room to talk rationally about their differences they will, given time and the right inducements, come out with peace. This just doesn't work, especially where the protagonists are in historic conflicts with complex roots and causes. We need to find models of being church that address this context and recognise that conflicts, like the poor, are always going to be with us. This has significant implications for how we understand reconciliation.

There are a million people in the north east of Ireland whose primary sense of communal self is British and who give political and cultural expression to their relationship to the peoples of Britain. They have been in Ireland for longer than all the non-indigenous peoples of North America. They are not blow-ins, it is their home and they belong. The belonging may be precarious,[8] but it is still a belonging to a place in which they conceive of themselves as British. Equally there are those in the north of the island of Ireland whose primary identity is Irish and for whom being in a political unit that is formally British is a source of conflict. Violence has not worked for either in removing their

8 John Dunlop, *A Precarious Belonging: Presbyterians and the Conflict in Ireland* (Blackstaff Press, 1995)

grievance or relocating the other. No one seems prepared to exchange identity for peace. To renegotiate identity in order to give space to the other and to reimagine the relationship between the conflicting groups is a viable task. But its resolution is essentially one of managing the identity conflict that will remain for the foreseeable future.

The other reality of being post-troubles is that all the churches in Northern Ireland, both leaders and members, are themselves victims of the trauma. We have lived through it, we have been shaped by it and it is impossible for any of us to act in a way that does not reflect the fact that the troubles are a major theme of our communal and personal story. Being a society at war with itself is part of our identity. This means that the church will get some things right and some things wrong. Christian believers, for all the spiritual resources available in Christ, are not immune from the shared experience of human community and this leads to painful contradictions in our witness. So we are post-troubles with all of the complexities that brings.

Post-Agreement but not Post-Agreeing

Terence McCaughey rightly reminds us that the Belfast Agreement of 1998 is not a reconciliation charter.

> *'...the Good Friday Agreement is not about reconciliation. It is about political accommodation – nothing more and certainly nothing less. There are things which a political accommodation cannot promise to deliver. It does not in itself involve anyone in acknowledging their responsibility for what went wrong. Much less does it call people or enable them to seek or grant forgiveness. Least of all does it promise reconciliation. That being said, however, its implementation might just nurture the conditions, social, political and economic under which reconciliation could take place.'* [9]

There currently exists a tendency in religious communities throughout the world to talk up the art of diplomacy and the art of political accommodation into the vision of reconciliation. In the

---

9 Writing in the *Irish Times*. Terence McCaughey is a Presbyterian minister and senior lecturer emeritus at Trinity College Dublin.

search for a moral political authority the temptation exists to translate political documents into sacred texts, an unwelcome reversal of the translation of sacred texts into political handbooks.

The Belfast Agreement and its political arrangements are flawed and parts of it do not work well, not only for Unionists but also for Republicans and Nationalists. There are ambiguities and processes that were the best that could be achieved in 1998 but need to now be renegotiated in the light of experience. Therefore the British and Irish governments back themselves into a corner by treating an essentially political document as if it was a reconciliation charter. Blocking any such necessary renegotiating is now as much a part of the problem of the current stalemate as the intransigence of those Unionists who have never accepted the Agreement in the first place.

There is a need to create space by recognising that while there is still a will for agreement amongst many people, within the Protestant and Unionist community the merits of the political accommodation of the Belfast Agreement are no longer credible. In ECONI's submission to the reconvened Dublin Forum for Peace and Reconciliation in January 2003[10] we emphasised this point. It is hard to see, given the failure of the current arrangements to convince many that the war is truly over, how we can avoid the need to renegotiate the terms on which we can learn to trust each other.

Dermot Nesbitt, a senior Unionist negotiator, defines politics not as the art of the possible, but the choice of the unpalatable over the unacceptable. Even as we engage in the noble task of reconciliation we need to learn the realism of living with that dilemma and to be able to discern between what is difficult to swallow and what is necessary to spew out of the body politic lest it poisons the whole.

Post-Christendom but not Post-Sectarian

The third observation about the context that I want to make is that we are post-Christendom, but not post-sectarian. To be post-Christendom means that the churches need to get real about the limit of their influence in society. The reality is that the people

---

10 ECONI statement: *Forum For Peace & Reconciliation* presented to the Forum for Peace and Reconciliation, Dublin Castle, January 2003 reprinted in Lion & Lamb Magazine Issue 34 Spring 2003.

who waged our war are, by and large, not people who belong to or attend church. In the most recent high profile sectarian encounters those engaging in picketing Holy Cross School, pipe bombing homes, attacking peaceful parades and provoking interface strife are not normally found in their churches on a Sunday. They don't give a damn what the church leaders say, they don't care.

We need to recognise that in a post-Christendom society what is said in the Kirk does not necessarily work on the street. Such *realpolitik* will change the way we understand how the church needs to function in the task of reconciliation and peacebuilding. Yet it remains true that for many the religious label is still a deep emotive force in their subconscious. Particularly within the Protestant community, whatever lack of religious observance there may be, the consequent religious prejudice towards and sheer hatred of Catholics shapes their conscious activity on the streets. And this is the insidious virus of sectarianism for which the community of faithful believers have to take some responsibility in their ministry of reconciliation.

REFLECTION

Let me now reflect on the church's function within the complexity of the Northern Ireland context. There are three areas where the church has operated in relating its witness to Christ to the communal conflict.

The Political function of the Church

It is part of the western disease that we have very short memories. We forget that until relatively recently in historical terms the context for politics, identity and belonging in most of Europe, never mind Northern Ireland, was shaped by religious understandings and ideas. Insightful scholars remind us that it was well into the 20th Century that British culture and even politics lost its roots in a religious context.[11] While the last century may have produced amazing social and political changes it is still but a blip in time, particularly for communities where the politics of identity have led to conflict and violence in a vicious circle of vengeance and revenge. Therefore we need to recognise we are living

? historical knowledge

11 For further reading see David Hempton, *Religion and Political Culture in Britain and Ireland: From the Glorious Revolution to the Decline of Empire* (Cambridge University Press, 1996) and Callum Brown, *The Death of Christianity in Britain* (Routledge 2000).

through a long process of dismantling the Christendom models that give people religious labels, ideology and context for their politics, identity and belonging.

Pope John XXIII in opening the second Vatican Council declared the age of Constantine over. Yet a mindset that has shaped the whole warp and woof of Christian theology and mission for 1500 years cannot be turned off with one council or a mere forty years of post-Vatican II history. Nor for that matter can it turn on the decision of Evangelical Protestants to think differently about how they relate faith to politics and to the public square in the context of a pluralist society. Because this cannot be switched off quickly we need to recognise that change is taking place at differing paces and in different ways in the lives of different communities.

The confusion of change around religious and political identity is profound. A leader of the Protestant Orange Order critiqued the Protestant church with the withering observation that the church had changed but didn't tell its people. That the enemy was now meant to be the friend was perplexing for those on the streets identifying with their religious communities and whose residual shared memory was of a church exhorting them to stand firm against papists and compromise.

With this in mind politically the church has functioned in three ways in Northern Ireland. There has been the overt politics of ***"God on our side"*** and this has not been the sole prerogative of the fundamentalists and conservative evangelicals. In the history of Ireland there is ample evidence to demonstrate how both the Catholic Church and Protestant churches across the theological spectrum have functioned with such a politicised model.

If anything the besetting sin of most Evangelical Protestants in Northern Ireland has not been the political model but the pietistic model of ***"God on my side"***, opting out of any sense of responsibility for what is happening beyond the boundaries of their own congregation or even their own life.

While we may lament the lack of prophetic voices in the church in Northern Ireland we cannot underestimate the impact of those willing to ask ***"who is on God's side?"*** Their voice has been present and they have been consistent from before the troubles right through to the present day. The evidence of this is to be found in a careful reading of the various documents and formal statements and reports emanating from the churches themselves and a myriad of interchurch bodies. There is no major church body that has not condemned the violence or that has not taken a stand for peace.

Alongside the formal prophetic role of the churches has been the ordinary people whose voice and unseen action has been raised against the brutality being carried on in their name in the community around them. It is William Blake who imagines sitting to dine with Isaiah and Ezekiel and discussing their prophetic certainty and courage. In response to his inquiry as to knowing when God has spoken, it is Isaiah who answers 'that the voice of honest indignation is the voice of God, I cared not for consequences, but wrote.' In simple, profound and unseen ways many church people, I believe, have been prophetic in our community through their honest indignation writ large in their actions and choices and so giving expression to the voice of God.

We have also learnt that being prophetic is not only a matter of speaking but it is also a matter of listening. For ECONI, strong on evangelical proclamation, it was through the gentle ministry Mennonite peacebuilder John Paul Lederach that we learnt this skill. Prophetic effectiveness in conflicts is rooted in where you sit; it is how you hear and how you identify with the people who are the protagonists. This brings me to the pastoral function of the church.

The Pastoral function of the Church

Churches in Northern Ireland have done an amazing job in ameliorating the effects of our conflict. The care and the cure of souls absorbed mass amounts of energy, especially for local clergy and pastors. We dare not undervalue the cost of attending to the emotional, spiritual and physical wounds of a congregation, burying the dead and all the while tending to your own trauma as part of a community in conflict. Indeed while others look to you to give meaning, purpose and security to the insecurity and disorder of the violence.

Like everyone else in 1970's and 80's Northern Ireland bomb scares and the latest report of death and destruction mark your daily routine. You too are affected; and the energy absorbed in just doing these things, pastorally holding the line, is immense and draining. And with that comes the guilt for not having the energy to dig out the spiritual resources, rise above circumstances and somehow act in this big beneficial manner of the church on behalf of everyone else.

The real heroes of Northern Ireland according to Mari Fitzduff, former Director of the Community Relations Council, are the milkmen, the postmen, the bread delivery men who, as the sun came up on the morning after the night before, went purposefully about their job. The clank of the post through the letterbox and the clink of the milk bottle on the doorstep signified normality was returning after the nightmare. Whatever had happened on your street, something of normal life was still sustained. The energy of hundreds of thousands of ordinary Christians, civil servants, public servants, GP's, casualty surgeons, nurses, teachers, business people and shop keepers - kept Northern Ireland going while determined terrorists sought to prove it ungovernable and to wreck it. Many did this because of their faith in God, a faith sustaining their energy to live out a deep spirituality. This ordinariness of the reconciling mission in the midst of real world conflict is something we should never underestimate.

One of the most potent examples of the pastoral role is the way the annual gatherings of many Protestant churches would begin by reading a list of those who had died as a result of the troubles in the previous year. Baptists in particular were notoriously pietistic in their response to the troubles, with what little formal reference to events outside the congregation being confined to the occasional prayer but rarely if ever any mention in the sermon. Yet, when the Baptist Union General Assembly met, a list of those Baptists who had so died was read.

It was in the context of such pastoral belonging that the church gained the right to mediate and to facilitate the peace. But this is to overstate the case. For it was individual clergy, often misunderstood across the divide and the focus of suspicion as those who had tended the wounds of the paramilitary community, who acted, often outside the approval of their church.

The Peacemaking function of the Church

This story is beginning to be told of the contribution of the church leaders to making peace in Northern Ireland. Protestant pastors have put themselves at risk acting as intermediaries with paramilitaries on behalf of those under threat. Catholic priests have given the last rites to British soldiers, most notoriously in the case of the two corporals executed by the IRA after driving into the route of a republican funeral. Wherever paramilitary feuds have broken out it has often been clergy who have acted as mediators. As prison chaplains they have visited and served those who organisations have been responsible for over 80% of the killings, building relationships of trust and respect.

The church, because of this pastoral belonging, was given a unique place to mediate and facilitate the peacemaking process. In a sense to be intimately engaged with the worst of what was happening inevitably means the pastor giving expression to the peacemaker. Indeed the church cannot be peacemaker unless it is prepared to understand the deep anxieties within its own community that produce the conflict.

The church has had an unsung peacemaking function in creating private space for political parties, paramilitaries and even the governments to find a way to engage with each other. In the peace process nearly every major contact and initiative that has produced fruit in bringing the violence to an end has been facilitated and nurtured by church people, Protestant and Catholic. This was no less true of the very first Provisional IRA cease-fires in the early 1970's. Even the secret MI6 dialogue with the IRA leadership had people of faith facilitating the contact.[12]

This has often been at great cost to those involved, not only in time and energy, but in verbal and occasionally physical attack, misunderstanding and being ostracised within their own communities, ecclesiastic and tribal. For it has to be admitted that the majority of this activity was informal and at best done with the knowledge of but not necessarily the sanction of church leaders.

The church has given public voice to the peace process through its ongoing commentary to its people and to the government. More importantly it has given public space in its buildings and in its organisations for the protagonists to finally begin to tentatively meet. The first meetings between Sinn Fein and Unionist Politicians on public platforms have, almost without exception,

12 The full story of how this was established in the early 1970's, kept in place and revitalised in the late 1980's is told by Peter Taylor in *The Brits: The War Against the IRA* (Bloomsbury, 2002)

taken place in church buildings or hosted by church organisations such as Corrymeela, ECONI and Glencree. In recent years local churches have organised political forums in their church halls at election time or at times of crisis, inviting local representatives from all the parties to meet and engage in political dialogue. This is a contribution that we must acknowledge and affirm.

Reconciliation

Where does this leave us in regard to our understanding of the reconciling mission of the church? Let me conclude with my reflections on reconciliation out of this experience.

We know in Northern Ireland that whatever our future holds it is a future that is going to be shared. Populations are not going to decamp and move, nor is there any immediate prospect of the breeding game reaching a decisive conclusion. The question is how we are going to share our future and what part does the *'R word'* have in that? Here I deliberately use the colloquial phrase some of us have adopted, as reconciliation has become the 'dirty' word of Northern Ireland politics. There are three things I think we need to bear in mind concerning this task of reconciliation.

The Critical Quest

First I want to affirm that reconciliation is a critical quest. I don't want to give up on it; to me it is central to the faith commitment of the church. Specifically it is core to any understanding of the Christian message and mission. Daniel Boyarin in his book on Paul and the politics of identity asks the question:

> "When Paul says, There is no Jew or Greek, no male and female in Christ, he is raising an issue with which we still struggle. Are they the particularities of human identity, the differences of value, or are they only an obstacle in the striving for justice and liberation?"[13]

This question goes to the heart of how we understand the Good News of God being in Christ, reconciling the world to Himself. This is a world of diversity, a world of connectedness and created order where the positive things that shape culture - belonging, place and custom - are part of how God made us. Yet as Liechty

---

13 Daniel Boyarin, *A Radical Jew: Paul and the Politics of Identity* (University of California Press, 1994) p.3.

and Clegg[14] show they so easily become distorted to produce sectarianism.

To belong to the space that we occupy geographically, to the time in which we are born, and to the community within which we are nurtured, are important aspects of the human experience. And the differences inherent to this embodied reality do have value. Indeed, they inform not only our natural state, but also our redeemed state. While being in Christ transforms us and transcends what we know when we journey beyond the dark glass of temporal existence, our eternal experiences of God remain rooted in a life lived in time, in a place and among a people.

In Revelation[15] we are presented with a biblical vision that around the throne of God people of every tribe, nation and language will be there to worship. So the reality of difference is recognised in the post-parousia state. The critical quest is how we hold those differences now in relation to each other and embrace diversity while overcoming the impulse of our fallen nature – to exclude and destroy on the basis of such diversity, to make a false god to worship of our tradition, land and people.

The Elusive Quest

Secondly, reconciliation is an elusive quest. Norman Porter[16] argues that a strong concept of reconciliation is needed for politics in Northern Ireland to work. Such reconciliation requires three things: fair interaction between citizens /members of opposing groups, that we overcome our antagonistic divisions by occupying common ground, and the presence of a society in which all citizens have a sense of belonging. It is our inability to agree on what constitutes fairness, to acknowledge common positions, and most critically to re-imagine a society in which we are all stakeholders, that makes our task so elusive.

I want to suggest that the elusiveness of reconciliation is not only political but is at heart a spiritual dilemma. Power and identity are the root cause of much human conflict, both interpersonal and communal. The Christian Gospel is a call to acknowledge Christ as the one to whom all power belongs and in

14 Joseph Liechty and Cecelia Clegg, *Moving Beyond Sectarianism: Religion, Conflict and Reconciliation in Northern Ireland* (Columba Press, 2001)

15 Revelation 7: 9,10

16 Norman Porter, *The Elusive Quest* (Blackstaff, 2003)

whom we find our true identity. Without a true conversion to Christ, in which we lay aside our claim to power and truly find ourselves in Christ, it is apparent that Christian reconciliation will always be elusive.

Honesty compels us to acknowledge that even within the community of faith true reconciliation is extremely rare. One of the exercises we ask church groups to complete is to compile a record of incidences of real reconciliation in their life and ministry within the last five years. Even extending the timescale to ten or fifteen years produces little change to the sparse list of examples. Often the attempt to reconcile is not made, partly due to the high tolerance level of conflict and breakdown within our churches, family and community. But of more interest is the increasing acknowledgement that tolerance itself is what often passes for reconciliation. We must acknowledge that this is indeed an important and critical step on the journey to reconciliation. Yet for many of us it has become the final and less costly destination.

There are places in our community where people have decided that, while interface violence is a social blight, they do not address it by reconciling their differences, they simply agree to put up a higher 'peace wall'.[17] We all know that often our churches do no more than agree to live within the bounds of tolerable difference on key matters of faith and practice. But we have not actually found our full reconciliation in Christ so that the world may know because we are one. Even in personal relationships we often hold back from a real place of reconciling encounter and 'live with' the friction within the bounds of the tolerable until it becomes a matter of intolerable differences. So there is a lot of tolerance masking as reconciliation and very little real reconciliation. For the stability of communities and relationships that may be no bad thing. But we need to be honest and recognise the elusiveness of this task of reconciling mission.

The Contingent Quest

That leads me to my final comment, reconciliation is always a contingent quest.

17 Belfast is known for its peace walls that provide a security barrier between adjacent Protestant and Catholic communities. These were initially erected from barbed wire by the British Army in 1969 and have now become a permanent and often landscaped feature at the key interfaces.

First there is an eschatological dimension to reconciliation. The reconciling mission of God in Christ is only completed in time and space with the parousia. There is a real danger, one to which activists are prone on a whole range of issues, of having an over realised eschatology as we seek the outworking of the prayer, your kingdom come, your will be done on earth as in heaven. How do we recognise the contingent nature implicit in the eschatological dimension of reconciliation when we are so passionate and committed to bearing witness to the ultimate truth that the coming kingdom represents? How do we acknowledge that for us it is Christ who is reconciling the world, a truth to which we bear witness, but which is complete only when the one in whom the created order is being made whole is revealed? How do we maintain this witness in the real world of flawed people with their fears and their anxieties without creating unrealistic expectations of politicians and frail human beings? In effect can we avoid the trap of promising more that we can credibly deliver from a biblical perspective?

Then there is a relational dimension to reconciliation that must take account of the complexity of human relationships. The capacity to forgive in Christian theology is intrinsically linked to the capacity to be forgiven. It is because we receive forgiveness that we can offer forgiveness and to receive we must recognise our need before God.

But the truth of this easily becomes distorted and dysfunctional. Indeed there is something perverted in looking to those bereaved by the violence of the powerful, either the terrorist or the state, to somehow moderate their desire for justice, out of a sense that all share responsibility for creating a society in which the conditions for violence exist. Yet that can often be how our desire to share responsibility for the context is heard and experienced.

In Northern Ireland we have people who are prepared to regret the necessity of having to use violence but not to apologise for the use of violence itself. To express remorse for the 'innocent' and 'unintended' victims, without awareness that those caught in a no warning car bomb in a busy shopping area fail to see the lack of intention. Regret that it was necessary is not the same thing as saying sorry, while many doubt it was ever necessary in the first place.

There is in truth no one model or process for every person or group caught up in the trauma of communal conflict. Each must find their way to address their particular legacy. And all will be at different places on that individual journey. To stress the need for peace and forgiveness in support of political stability and national reconciliation risks devaluing both the trauma and the integrity of those whose journey towards reconciliation is no less sincere by the demands they place on truth and justice. For this reason alone we must always recognise the contingent nature to our mission of reconciliation.

And there is a dimension to reconciliation that goes to the heart of our differences in theology, spirituality and liturgy. Public expression of remorse, regret and even repentance needs a shared framework within which the act of contrition is received and made effective for both the victim and perpetrator. Differences in Catholic and Evangelical Protestant approaches to the communal dealing with sin, confession and reconciliation, whether for the present or for the past, means that there does not exist in reality a common spiritual context in which to facilitate any public acts of reconciliation. And until we can find not only the language, but the redemptive and healing context in which to talk to each other about the hurt we have suffered and caused, then our efforts towards reconciliation will always be contingent.

Critical it may be, but reconciliation is profoundly elusive and contingent. The temptation to deploy it as yet another resource in the toolbox of international statecraft, or even to enhance the effective mission of the church, must be resisted. Instead it is a fragile species in a hostile environment, requiring careful and skilful tending.

Bearing Witness

I have chosen to reflect on reconciliation under the theme of bearing witness to the overcomer of violence, rather than the theme of overcoming violence, reconciling mission. The tone implicit in the former is I believe truer to our task and struggle as disciples of Christ and citizens of the kingdom of God.

As in our personal identity, both nature and nurture play a role in forming the character of the church. We are a people who are in Christ and in, but not of, the world. It is part of our nature as Christians, our genetic spiritual makeup, that we are to be a reconciling community bringing in the kingdom of God. We are 'born again' as children of God and nurtured in the new humanity of the kingdom community to which we now belong.

And yet our human nature means that our nurture is also as frail human beings, with an incarnational belonging in communities that are struggling with deep seated and complex issues of self-definition and belonging, centred around the threat of the existence of the other. The church cannot remove itself from this fallen human experience. It shares in it and it is shaped by it.

Knowing the divine nature and nurture of the church does not, in my experience, resolve this tension with our human nature and nurture as fallen people. In a world of conflict we are a people in a conflict of eternal consequences. The tension and struggle experienced by Christians in this place of conflict leads me to conclude that we need to be modest in our claims of overcoming violence or of reconciliation in the mission of the church today.

THEOLOGIES OF MISSION AS CATALYSTS FOR VIOLENCE – A CASE STUDY

Drew Gibson

Introduction

Throughout the history of the Christian Church mission and violence have often gone hand in hand. Frequently missionaries have been the objects of violence from those who oppose them but tragically, violence has also been perpetrated by those engaged in mission. In both cases the theology of mission that has driven the missionaries must be held partly responsible for the subsequent violence. Violence has been directed at missionaries for three reasons. First, some violence has been directed at missionaries because the sad truth is that sin sometimes responds to the grace of God with violent antagonism; second there is violence directed at missionaries who have unwittingly provoked such a reaction through ignorance or naïve enthusiasm but third, sometimes missionaries have unwittingly provoked a violent reaction by wicked missionary activities, driven by an aberrant theology of mission. Secondly, when we consider violence as springing out of missionary theology (and consequent missionary activity) we can think of the Crusades[1], *encomiendas*[2] and possibly even the recent Iraq conflict[3]. These are well known but my point is more subtle. It is the contention of this essay that the traditional Evangelical theology of mission in Northern Ireland has made conflict inevitable and that this theology has not only failed to address the physical violence that has been endemic in the Province for generations but has actually contributed to its continuance.

Four preliminary comments: I do not want to suggest that a coherent theology of mission has been responsible for the violence in general or even for particular acts of violence in Northern Ireland. I simply want to argue that the particular Evangelical theology of mission common in Northern Ireland has been an

1 S.C. Neill, *A History of Christian Missions* (Pelican, 1964) pp.113-116
2 S.C. Neill, *Ibid*, p.170
3 http://www.guardian.co.uk/Iraq/Story/0,2763,929399,00.html

unwitting contributor to a situation in which violence has been actively embraced by a few, tacitly supported by many and often accepted as the 'least worst option' by the great majority.

Second, my comments here are on a particular type of Evangelical mission theology. Not all Evangelicals subscribe to the theology below, although, if I had been writing this essay twenty years ago, I could have said everything without this qualification. I recognise that the work of ECONI[4] and of many individual Evangelicals is rooted in a much more appropriate theology of mission.

Third, while I will be offering a negative critique of traditional Evangelical mission theology in Northern Ireland, this should not be interpreted as a blanket criticism of this theology. I believe that it has much to commend it. I am restricting my comments to those aspects that have unwittingly made it a catalyst for violence in the Province.

What then is the relationship between the violence in Northern Ireland and the traditional Evangelical theology of mission in the Province?

1. Mission as a distraction from violence.

Among Evangelicals in Northern Ireland the word 'mission' is still commonly used in the two senses familiar to Evangelicals and other Christians in past generations. First, it means that which the Church in the 'West' does in the rest of the world. This type of mission has been a welcome distraction for some from the problem of cross community reconciliation. Some Evangelicals have been passionate about mission in the farthest parts of the world, including issues of social justice and yet have ignored similar situations on their own doorstep. This is not surprising as it is often much easier to help in someone else's problems than to make changes and grasp nettles in an attempt to solve one's own problems. This has been mission by displacement in which Samaria and the ends of the earth have been a substitute for Jerusalem and Judea. So Evangelical theology of mission's first contribution to violence in Northern Ireland is that it has taken attention away from the problem and been a means of spiritual escapism.

4 Evangelical Contribution on Northern Ireland see further: http://www.econi.org/

2. Mission is the same as evangelism.

When considering the witness of the Church within Northern Ireland, traditional Evangelicals have seen evangelism and mission as virtually synonymous. This has meant that traditional Evangelicals have expected that their contribution as Christians to society should be to evangelise that society. Therefore, until relatively recently, Evangelical social action was conspicuous by its absence. This meant that the social inequalities between Protestants and Catholics that had characterised the Province since its birth did not come within the purview of mission. It was these inequalities that gave birth to the violence of the late sixties. If traditional Evangelicals had understood the addressing of social inequalities to be something to which God calls His people they would have been a positive influence in the People's Democracy movement rather than being numbered among those who threw stones at them at Burntollet Bridge[5].

Further, traditional Evangelicals have set the verbal proclamation of the Gospel over against social concern, the latter being seen as at best a distraction from and at worst a completely inadequate substitute for the former. All Evangelicals would agree that, in theory, abolishing violence is a good thing. But traditional Evangelical thinking maintains that in the case of Northern Ireland the good can be the enemy of the best. If abolishing violence is to be done at the expense of preaching the Gospel, then it is to sell out the eternal in favour of the temporal, which can never be acceptable. In addition, peacemakers have often been those who have been associated with the liberal wing of the Church, with Ecumenicals, with advocates of the 'Social Gospel' all of which are terms of abuse in traditional Northern Irish Evangelicalism. Therefore these peacemakers have been rejected as 'unsound', even as a fifth column. To associate with such is to break the principle of separation. Therefore, addressing violence as an aspect of doing mission is inconceivable.

3. Mission and Anti-Catholicism.

The dualistic worldview of traditional Evangelicals has maintained hostility towards the Roman Catholic Church as an absolute necessity. The Catholic Church is not a true church, it is a synagogue of Satan and therefore fidelity to Christ demands

---

5 F. Lyons, *Ireland Since the Famine (*Fontana, 1973) p.764

hostility towards the Satanic opponent of the Gospel. It is equally obvious that hostility from Catholics towards Evangelicals should be understood as hostility to the Gospel[6]. On the basis of this understanding, violence is inevitable and reconciliation impossible. While mainstream Evangelicals have not regularly espoused physical violence, other than the violence of the state security forces, most have understood that violence is to be expected from the forces of evil and especially from those forces of evil supported by, or indeed, organised by Rome[7]. To stand against such is one's Christian duty[8]. However, concern for the salvation of the individual Catholic should make one all the more committed to evangelism among Catholics.

Further, traditional Evangelical self understanding accepts and rejoices in 'persecution for the sake of the Gospel'[9] because Scripture presents this as the norm. Jesus proclaimed the Kingdom and was crucified, Peter preached and was imprisoned, Stephen bore witness and was stoned and Paul was regularly brutally treated on his travels. Further, the history of the Church is the story of a similar pattern of faithful Gospel proclamation followed by persecution and figures such as Tyndale, Hus, Latimer and Ridley and more recently, Jim Eliot are taken as models[10]. Evangelicals in Northern Ireland have always understood themselves to be victims of violence rather than perpetrators. This violence has been seen as a necessary price to pay for fidelity to Christ and as such it validates their life and witness. Such an understanding of this historic connection between violence and mission sees attempts to avoid violence as cowardice or infidelity or apostasy, to be shunned by those who are true witnesses.

Evangelicals have seen Catholics as, by definition, objects of evangelism.

Traditional Northern Irish Evangelicals believe that Catholics, as children of the Whore of Babylon, cannot possibly be Christians and hence are, without exception, objects of evangelism. Believing that many individual Catholics are deluded, having been brainwashed by the Church of Rome, traditional Northern Irish

---

6 M. Hill, *The Time of the End* (Belfast Soc. 2001) p.51f

7 S. Bruce, *God Save Ulster* (OUP 1986) p.222

8 M. Hill, op. cit, p.53

9 cf. Matt. 5:10f

10 G. Jordan, *Not of This World* (Blackstaff, Belfast, 2001) p.194

Evangelicals can talk of loving Catholics while hating the Catholic Church. This utterly ignores the deep affection that even nominal Catholics have for the Church[11]. Messages of love towards individuals are drowned out by vitriol poured out against the institution beloved by those individuals. It is hardly surprising that Catholics respond with deep hostility towards those who insult their 'Mother'. As part of this response, violence is not far away.

Evangelical understanding of the universal applicability of the Gospel has been confused with the expression of the Gospel in culturally variable terms.

Traditional Northern Irish Evangelicals have presented the Gospel as a cultural and social package that has included such things as political opinions, musical tastes, sporting pursuits, places to live and schools to attend. Thus the Gospel is commonly perceived by both sides to be closely related to Britishness and Unionism[12]. This is made more difficult because Catholics have traditionally perceived this Britishness and Unionism to be oppressive and unjust. Consequent anti-British violence has been perceived by many traditional Evangelicals as inseparable from and even identifiable with anti-Gospel violence.

A particular example of this cultural confusion is attitudes to the Bible. In many parts of the English speaking world some traditional evangelicals understand the King James Version of the Bible to carry a unique divine blessing, especially in evangelism. On the contrary, most non-Christians see the use of the KJV as an anachronism that shows how out of date the Church is. In Northern Ireland this situation is made worse by the understanding by both communities that the KJV carries a royal warrant and so its use has political overtones. This, among many other things, has contributed to the feeling of culturally Irish Catholics that the evangelistic efforts of Evangelicals are a threat to their identity and culture, even to their existence. Not surprisingly, with the history of the relationship between Britain and Ireland being what it is, this perception has been enfolded into the rationale for Republican violence. Just as Evangelicals feel threatened by absorption into an Irish Republic dominated by Catholicism[13] so Catholics feel

---

11 F. Boal, M. Keane, D. Livingstone, *Them and Us* (Inst. of Irish Studies, 1997) p.29f
12 A. Thomson (Ed), *Faith in Ulster* (ECONI, Belfast, 1996) p.65
13 Boal et al. *op. cit.* p.139

threatened by being part of a Province dominated by Protestants[14]. For both communities a violent response is never far below the surface.

The traditional Catholic linkage between salvation and the Church as an institution has been seen by many Protestants as a threat to all that they hold dear.

The links between the Catholic Church and Irish republican terrorism are by no means straightforward, except in the minds of many traditional Northern Irish Evangelicals. To them the link is simple. The Catholic Church wants to destroy Protestantism and embrace all people within the grasp of its false salvation; it has already done this in the Republic of Ireland and the Nationalist desire for a united Ireland is the obvious next step[15]. Therefore Rome supports and facilitates Republican terrorism in order to achieve this end. It is absolutely essential for traditional Evangelicals to stand against this demonic mission[16]. How then can one talk about reconciliation and the ending of violence? The struggle in Northern Ireland is made even more important when the Province is trumpeted as the last bastion of true evangelicalism in the world (it is not only Northern Irish Evangelicals who believe this[17]). Therefore violence may also be aroused in Protestants who fear Rome. If Rome is the great enemy, then it is right to destroy her and her acolytes. The destruction of that which is 'anti-Christ' is clearly a missionary endeavour and traditional Northern Irish Evangelicals have been guilty of condoning destruction by violent means. Perhaps the only surprise is that more priests and nuns have not been the objects of Protestant violence. Maybe the respect for the clergy that is still part of Northern Irish society has always been strong enough to keep the clergy safe.

4. Mission as an occasional activity.

Evangelical understanding of mission as a periodic activity of the Church, often done by specialists, has produced 'in your face' activities that have increased the feeling of threat among Catholics. In traditional Northern Irish Evangelical circles the word 'mission'

---

14 *Ibid*, p.64f

15 Opsahl Commission in A. Thompson (Ed), *The Great White Tent* (ECONI, Belfast 1999) p.26

16 A. Thompson (Ed), *Faith in Ulster* p.84f

17 See for example http://www.lisburn.com/books/americas-debt/american-debt.htm

can still refer to a specific campaign of evangelism. Such campaigns are common in Northern Ireland. Often they are well advertised and generously funded. Consider how they might be perceived by a Northern Irish Catholic. On his way to work he sees billboards advertising the campaign; through his letter box he receives an invitation to this series of meetings; a workmate might invite him to the same series of meetings and even when he listens to the local radio stations he may well hear the same invitation repeated a number of times. In a park close to his home he sees a large white marquee with hundreds of people flooding in, all of whom he knows to be hostile to him and his Church. With all of the overtones noted above, how can he feel anything but threatened? It can come as no surprise that a minority of those who feel threatened respond with violence. Traditional Northern Irish Evangelicals would be appalled at the thought that their evangelistic missions might indirectly give rise to violence, yet I believe that this is an inescapable conclusion.

5. Mission vocabulary.

Violent, military metaphors have been unhelpful in making associations between the Gospel and violence. The Christian faith and mission in particular have often been presented in violent terms. *Fighting the good fight, soldiers of the cross, the sword of the Spirit* and *spiritual warfare* are common motifs and have been common currency for generations. I would not wish to deny the validity of these motifs and it is obvious that in many missionary contexts they are entirely appropriate. But, traditional Evangelicals in Northern Ireland make the tacit assumption that, if an idea is in the Bible, then that alone is justification for its indiscriminate use. This is very unwise in places like Northern Ireland where these motifs have provided a vocabulary that has been very much at home in the apologetic for sectarian violence[18].

A Note on Future directions

1. A theology of mission based firmly on the Biblical understanding of the atonement as reconciliation would obviously be appropriate. An understanding of evangelism as reconciliation between God and individual human beings would come to the fore and a suitably derived evangelistic

18 M. Hill, *op. cit.* p.53

methodology could be developed. This would allow a thoroughly Biblical theology of evangelism to flow naturally into a programme of social involvement of which peacemaking would be an integral part.

2. A look at the Liberation model for doing theology might be very useful. From there we could learn much. For example, embracing commitment to Christ and commitment to the poor as a first step can integrate a theology of conversion with an appropriate theology of social involvement. Developing a Northern Irish Utopian vision based on Scriptural eschatology could give a sense of direction for the Church's work of seeking conversion of individuals in parallel with the conversion of the social order. Prayerful, honest reflection, in the light of Scripture, on the failed praxis of the past is essential. The ordinary Christian who, in Evangelical circles is already probably a member of a 'base ecclesial community,' must be fully engaged in missiological reflection as an honoured contributor.

3. In contrast to the rest of the world perhaps, the concept of *Missio Dei* is by no means past its 'sell by date'; it is of crucial importance. An understanding of God's total purpose for his world must be our starting point. From this, our theology of mission must be freshly derived and fully contextualised, not bought in ready made from elsewhere or preserved from the past and reheated.

Conclusion

In conclusion, I hope that what I have said may help to explain one aspect of why Northern Ireland, with its high percentage of committed Christians, has experienced such social turbulence for so long. A traditional Evangelical theology of mission has its faults but in many parts of the world it has done and can do sterling service. This is not so in Northern Ireland. If we are to address our problems we will have to address our theology of mission. We will have to rethink our definitions and vocabulary in the hope that this will have an effect on our activities and methods. A thoroughly contextualised, locally relevant, theology of mission is crucial if Evangelicals are to adequately address violence in the Province. It will not be the whole answer but at least it might remove some obstacles to peace and reconciliation.

MALAWI

IDENTITY POLITICS AND THE GRACE OF GOD

"I Have Seen the Lion Lie down with the Lamb"

Kenneth R Ross

Ethnic Conflict and the Gospel of Christ

Conflict between two ethnic communities was the dominant feature of life in northern Malawi when the Livingstonia Mission began work there in the 1880s.[1] The Tonga people who lived along the shore of Lake Malawi found themselves facing an immigrant people – the Ngoni who had originally been refugees from the Zulu Empire of Shaka but who now asserted themselves as an aggressive, military people. Ngoni raids on Tonga villages and the inevitable Tonga reprisals provided the political context in which the Scottish missionaries began their work of proclaiming the gospel of Christ. Theirs was a precarious position since, if they became inadvertently identified with one side or the other, they could very easily be drawn into the conflict themselves. So they lived dangerously but they persevered.

Once they had begun to learn the language, one of their first tasks was Bible translation. At first all they could manage were a few selected passages. One of their choices was the passage in Isaiah 11 which sets forth the vision of the end of all violence and destruction – a time when wolves and sheep would live happily together and when the lion would lie down with the lamb. One day the attempt to translate this passage was read to a gathering of Tonga smallholders and fisherfolk. Now, unlike most of us, these Tonga people knew lions and they knew lambs. Lion and lamb lying down together – that could never be! There could be nothing more absurd. "These missionaries are definitely crazy – imagine anyone talking such nonsense!" So this first attempt at a Bible

1 See John McCracken, *Politics and Christianity in Malawi 1875-1940: The Impact of the Livingstonia Mission in the Northern Province*, Cambridge: Cambridge University Press, 1977, 2nd ed. Blantyre: CLAIM, 2000.

translation went down as a huge joke among the Tonga people and they had many laughs at the expense of the missionaries.

As time went on, however, both Tonga and Ngoni became ever more interested in the message which the missionaries preached and the time came when some were baptised and began to form worshipping congregations. One day a number of congregations came together for a communion service. On one side of the minister sat an elder of the Tonga people, so recently raided; and on the other an elder from among the Ngoni, the proud warrior people. "As the service proceeded, one man in the congregation was twitching with excitement. As soon as the benediction was spoken and the people rose to go, he rushed among his friends crying, 'Today I have seen it. With these two very eyes of mine. Yes, now I have seen it. He was right.' 'What have you seen, brother?' they demanded. 'I have seen the lion lie down with the lamb.'"[2]

This sense of reconciliation and the new identity, which it forged, is reflected in some of the hymns which were composed by the first generation of Ngoni Christians. Still sung in Malawi today is the great hymn of Peter Thole which includes these lines:

> Leap up my soul; leap up and sing
> Take heart again; here comes your king.
> Redemption done by God's right hand
> Is breaking forth *through all the land.*
>
> Dance, dance my heart; rejoice and sing
> This is the morning of the king.
> Break forth in praise, let men declare
> The dawn is breaking *everywhere.*[3]

This expansive and unifying vision was a response to the Christian message. It broke through geographical distances and historical differences to give people a sense of belonging together, united by the momentous event of the coming of the gospel of Christ. Without losing or compromising their locality or ethnicity,

---

2 Fergus Macpherson, *North of the Zambezi: A Modern Missionary Memoir*, Edinburgh: The Handsel Press, 1998, pp.169-70.

3 Fergus Macpherson, "*Sumu za Chifipa*: Christian Songs in Malawi", *Bulletin of the Scottish Institute of Missionary Studies*, Vol. 6-7 (1990-91), p.52; see also Kenneth R. Ross, *Christianity in Malawi: A Sourcebook*, Gweru: Mambo Press, 1996, pp.49-67.

people opened themselves to a wider sense of belonging and embraced a redefined identity. This was a powerful force for reconciliation.

Identity Politics and Contemporary Conflicts

Not so long ago, such tales of warring tribes being reconciled through receiving the Christian gospel seemed very dated. Today they suddenly have a very contemporary ring. Sources of identity which were suppressed during the bi-polar era of the Cold War have re-surfaced with a vengeance in the course of the 1990s. As Michael Ignatieff comments: "The key narrative of the new world order is the disintegration of nation states into ethnic civil war; the key architects of that order are warlords; and the key language of our age is ethnic nationalism."[4] Tribal warfare is no longer at a distance either historically or geographically. Rather it appears to be thriving in today's conditions. While a conflict may present itself as a struggle between two intransigent ethnic or religious groups, it is necessary to recognise that there are invariably deeper forces at work.

Whatever may be the local factors in creating a situation of conflict, there is the underlying global reality of what the United Nations Development Programme describes as "parallel worlds".[5] There is security, affluence and power in the one; violence, poverty and disintegration in the other. In the situation of increasing deprivation in which many communities find themselves in today's world, ethnic and/or religious identity can often become a rallying point in the struggle for survival.[6] Such sources of identity can also be exploited by unscrupulous politicians in order to secure

---

4 Michael Ignatieff, *Blood and Belonging: Journeys into the New Nationalism*, London: BBC Books and Chatto & Windus, 1993, p.2.

5 United Nations Development Programme, *Human Development Report*, New York and Oxford: Oxford University Press, 1999, p.1.

6 In identity politics it is often difficult to disentangle religious and ethnic components. As Scott Appleby comments: "The distinctions between religion and ethnicity as bases for nationalism are seldom clear in practice. In many settings the two are intertwined and mutually reinforcing. Religion can provide a supernatural justification for mundane ethnic claims, lending them an eternal (and thus non-negotiable) aura. Likewise, ethnic society is often the very soil in which the otherwise lifeless seed of religion is planted and takes root.... Many of these conflicts are called 'ethnoreligious' because it is virtually impossible to disaggregate the precise roles of religion and ethnicity." R. Scott Appleby, *The Ambivalence of the Sacred: Religion, Violence and Reconciliation*, Lanham and Oxford: Rowman and Littlefield, 2000, p.61.

their own power or advance their own agendas. As a result, the growth of an exclusive global economy has been accompanied by an explosion of civil wars, genocide and ethnic cleansing. Identity politics is the dynamite which, under such conditions, ignites inter-communal conflict.

As identity politics provokes conflict, causing untold suffering around the world, how can Christian faith give practical expression to the reconciliation of which the gospel speaks?

1) Relativization of Identity and Reconciliation of Communities

The Bible recognises the nations or ethnic communities which mark human society. Indeed it is all *nations* who are to be made disciples.[7] Yet when nations claim an absolute loyalty they become idols and have to be cut down to size. Christian mission does its work within this dialectic of *affirming* national and ethnic identity as the sphere within which Christ becomes known and enfleshed, while always *relativizing* it as incomplete in itself and finding its destiny in the wider purpose of God which embraces all peoples and draws them together before the throne of the Lamb.[8] It says both "yes" and "no " to the claims of the nations. *Yes*, they are valued and loved by God and called to discipleship in and through Jesus Christ. But, *no*, they can never have the absolute loyalty which we owe to God alone and, *no*, their ultimate destiny is not found in themselves but in the wider purpose of God in which they are called to have a part.

As Christoph Schwoebel comments: "Over against our solidarity as sinners and our calling to be one in Christ these distinctions [of class, nation, culture, race or sex] have at best a penultimate and relative value. Their value is relative to the reality of reconciliation which is promised to us in the gospel. This relativization of political, national, cultural, ethnic and racial absolutes is one of the most important implications of the message of reconciliation."[9]

The Church's mission constantly drives it to become fully local, rooted in the native soil of each particular community – what

---

7 See Matthew 28:19.

8 Cf. N.T. Wright, *The New Testament and the People of God*, (Christian Origins and the Question of God Vol. 1) London: SPCK, 1992, pp.448-49.

9 Christoph Schwoebel, "Reconciliation: From Biblical Observations to Dogmatic Reconstruction", in Colin E. Gunton ed., *The Theology of Reconciliation*, London & New York: T. & T, Clark, 2003, p.37.

mission studies refers to as indigenization. Yet it is also ever conscious of its catholic or universal character, that it is part of a community of faith whose scope is global and whose intention is to reach out to the whole of humanity. This gives the church the capacity both to affirm the integrity of national and ethnic identities but always to de-absolutize them and to lead them to find their purpose and destiny in a wider community to which many others bring the wealth of their histories, cultures, languages and modes of thought.[10] "The distance born out of allegiance to God and God's future," writes Croatian theologian Miroslav Volf, "creates space in us to receive the other."[11] Through active partnership in mission this vital reality comes to life within the church. We are able to appreciate the glorious diversity of a multi-ethnic world while discovering the common belonging in a wider community of faith which sets our own ethnic identity in its true perspective. This can be a very significant building block in the resolution of ethnically-based conflict.

2) Partnership in Mission: Recovering a Common Belonging

Underlying ethnically-based conflict is the economic disparity between the affluent and the impoverished which creates the conditions in which people turn in desperation to destructive identity politics. Here, there is need to point beyond the paradigm of protective security to the Christian vision of mutual dependency and vulnerability in which security and hope for all may be sustained. To do so in today's world means stubbornly, tirelessly working at the church-to-church partnerships which hold together brothers and sisters in Christ across the divide. The greater the economic divide between North and South, however, the more difficult it becomes to express partnership meaningfully. John Hull has stated the difficulty in this way: "The iron curtain has passed away and even the bamboo curtain hardly exists, but the place has been taken by the money curtain. We in the two-seventh rich world are surrounded by a money curtain which is like a one-way mirror. It is invisible to those of us on the inside because we can see right through it, but to the poor majority outside the money curtain it stands as a glittering barrier through which they cannot

10 Cf. Michael W. Payne, "Identity and Global Ethnic Violence: A Theological-Missiological Reflection", *Mission Studies*, Vol. XIX-2, 38 (2002), pp.113-135.

11 Miroslav Volf, *Exclusion and Embrace: A Theological Exploration of Identity, Otherness and Reconciliation*, Nashville: Abingdon, 1996, p.51.

pass. We can go to them but they cannot come to us."[12] Making partnerships work across such a barrier can often seem a thankless task. Yet is it not our calling to witness to the one who has destroyed the barrier, the dividing wall of hostility? Do we not have to point to a curtain that is torn apart from top to bottom?

Elusive, fragile, vulnerable as it is, there is a reality delineated in the concept of partnership in the gospel which takes us into the heart of what it means to be Christ's. Indeed, while admittedly it too often remains at the level of lip service, it gives the opportunity to discover the true cost of discipleship. To enter into partnership in the gospel with another church is to be prepared to offer meaningful presence and solidarity at the worst of times as well as at the best of times. Only through such active witness to its faith can the church offer hope to the world of our time. In the context of the "war against terrorism" it is often pointed out that it is the underlying causes of terrorism – poverty, injustice, ecological degradation – which need to be combated. Drain the swamp and there will be no more mosquitoes! In South Africa the point has been well made that talk of reconciliation is hollow if it is not founded upon the struggle for economic justice.[13] It is here that the partnership in the gospel, which brings together in common commitment those on either side in our divided world, may be seed for solutions to the deepest causes of conflict in our time. By aligning itself, through partnership, with the most excluded and most disadvantaged sections of the global community, sharing their life and speaking with them and for them, the church points to the reconciliation in Christ which is the hope of the world.

It is this kind of partnership, sometimes sustained over generations, which breaks through the invisible curtain between the "parallel worlds". Perhaps it finds its most powerful expression in contexts where mission partners serve together in multi-ethnic teams or communities. Their deep engagement with one another forms the kind of human bridge which can link churches, cultures and civilisations through faith in Jesus Christ.

---

12 John M. Hull, "Mission, Education and Globalisation", Churches Commission on Mission Annual Conference papers, Durham, Sept 2000.

13 See David Mosoma, "Economic Reconciliation: Foundation for a Just Society", *Journal of Black Theology in South Africa*, Vol. 11/2 (1997), pp.64-80; R.T.H. Dolamo, "Reconciliation and Economic Justice in South Africa: The Role of the Church and Theology", *Voices from the Third World*, Vol. 22/1 (1999), pp.85-96.

Furthermore, far from creating another exclusive, polarising community, the experience of discovering the identity of others through shared mission commitment tends to function as preparation and training for encounter with those who belong to other faith communities.[14] By cultivating deep personal relationships which transcend every human demarcation and division, Christian mission generates both the bonds and the skills needed to make reconciliation a visible and potent reality.

3) The Surprise Factor: God's Grace

So many people have been hurt and wounded by the raging conflicts of our time that something truly radical is needed before there can be any hope of healing and reconciliation. When great wrongs have been perpetrated it may be that retributive justice is not enough to set things right. There is need to find what Desmond Tutu has called, "the difficult but ultimately rewarding path of destroying enemies by turning them into friends".[15] In the final analysis, this is the path of God's grace. It is grace which ever surprises us because it is unexpected and unmerited. "Not diminished but rather fulfilled through self-limitation, God stoops to endure and thus to heal and conquer the most broken, terminal conditions of the human tragedy."[16] Amazing grace! This is what grips us in Jesus Christ and gives us a capacity for forgiveness and reconciliation which we would otherwise never find in ourselves. When all human efforts to resolve an intractable conflict have been exhausted, there can be the surprise of God's grace – opening up a possibility that no one had thought was there.

Narratives of hatred and vengeance are aplenty. The church is charged to offer a counter-narrative of grace, forgiveness and reconciliation. As John Webster comments: "Human acts of reconciliation are in accordance with the structure of reality which God in Christ creates and to the existence of which the gospel testifies; and therefore they are acts which tend towards the true end of creation that God's reconciling act establishes once and for all in Christ's reconciling person and work."[17] Rooted in the

---

14 Cf. D. Preman Niles, "Toward the Fullness of Life: Intercontextual Relationships in Mission", *International Review of Mission*, Vol. XCI No. 363 (October 2002), pp.471-82.

15 Desmond Tutu, *No Future Without Forgiveness*, London: Rider, 1999, p.138.

16 Alan E. Lewis, *Between Cross and Resurrection: A Theology of Holy Saturday*, Grand Rapids: Eerdmans, 2001, p.173.

17 John Webster, "The Ethics of Reconciliation", in Gunton, *The Theology of Reconciliation*, p.117

experience of God's grace, the church can offer space for truth, for justice, for healing, for new possibilities. Under Archbishop Tutu's chairmanship, the South African Truth and Reconciliation Commission was able to offer such space within a very public forum. Perhaps it is only under the shadow of God's grace that it is possible.

Confidence in the grace of God is grounded in the reality of Jesus Christ. The Christ who enters the life of a community is the same Jesus Christ who so opened himself to others as to die for them. The cross, planted at the core of the community, moves it to find its identity not in asserting itself over against others but rather in the vulnerability of being radically open to them. To a world where untold violence arises from the self-assertion of individuals and communities, the life of faith is one where, in the words of the apostle Paul, "*I* have been crucified with Christ and *I* no longer live, but Christ lives in me".[18] This great paradox that it is in losing our life that we gain it, that it is in death that we find life, is the key to reconciliation. For it both affirms who we are and impels us to open ourselves to others and to find our future with them. As David Stevens comments: "We are able to make space for the other because Christ has made space for us. While we are made one in Christ particular identities are not abolished but they are relativised and subordinated. This new identity in Christ leaves no room for individual or collective claims of superiority or self-righteousness. Reconciliation in Christ is about being freed from anxiety about identity. We do not have to shore up our own selfhood or self-esteem. We are to trust in the goodness and grace of God."[19]

The new centre found in Jesus Christ, writes Miroslav Volf, "opens the self up, makes it capable and willing to give itself for others and to receive others in itself."[20] As nations and peoples are discipled, they express themselves in the kind of self-giving love in which Christ found his identity and purpose and in which our world may find true hope today. The way of Christ tells us, writes Alan Lewis, that "trust, defencelessness, and vulnerability are in themselves, despite all appearances, finally more productive and

---

18 Galatians 2:20

19 David Stevens, "A Time to Heal: Perspectives on Reconciliation and Overcoming Violence", *Connections* Vol. 6 (2002) No 2, p.32.

20 Volf, *Exclusion and Embrace*, p.71.

protective than all stratagems for aggression or defence, attack or retaliation, self-assertion or self-protection." Following Christ means being willing "to lead risky, unprotected, costly lives, open to others and committed to self-expenditure on their behalf."[21] It is because they share this faith-perspective that churches working together as partners in mission have such great potential in the resolution of conflict and the achievement of reconciliation.

Conclusion

Christian mission today might seem just as unlikely to be a force for reconciliation in inter-communal conflict as did the Scottish missionaries among the Tonga and Ngoni in the 1880s. Yet in the gospel there are resources to relativize every human source of identity, to reach across every division through active partnership, and to witness to the healing and transformation found in God's grace. Could there be any more convincing demonstration of the authentic meaning of Christian mission today than to live out the elements of the gospel which make for reconciliation among divided and hostile communities?

21 Lewis, *Between Cross and Resurrection*, pp.321, 454.

NICARAGUA

GETTING BEYOND VIOLENCE: "AFTER THE CEASE-FIRE" OBSERVED

Margaret Raven

LOOKING OUT

Researching, communicating, telling and disseminating an accurate picture of the sweep of history in a nation is a prerequisite for visioning a future. *The future is never, what we ourselves long for. It is never what we have been expecting.*

In 1989 in Nicaragua (Central America) the ten-year civil war ended with the Sandinista and Contra soldiers filing past Cardinal Miguel Obando y Bravo and laying down their arms. Almost everyone wanted peace. Whether they were the oligarchy who had migrated to Paris, Geneva or Los Angeles or the humbler urban people or peasants from the rural areas who migrated away from the war to Los Angeles, Houston and Washington D.C. USA - they had longed for peace so that they could return to their homeland. Whether they were the marxist intellectuals of the left, the military leadership of the right and the left, the socialist cadres or the cautiously neutral - all who had been resident in Nicaragua over the last ten to fifteen years - they longed for a negotiated peace, elections, stable government and a continuation of building the future by peaceful means. A return to normality was victory.

"A return to normality" was the consciously apolitical phrase used following ceasefire. Many soldiers were reluctant to go back to civilian life: fear of reprisals was one factor. There was no work, they would be a financial burden on their family, their family might not want them back - they did not know. The youngest guerrilla of the left and the right had maybe two years of primary school, military skills and, survival skills. They were young women and men with a vision: independent and consciously modern. They had no intention of returning home to the old-fashioned ways and authoritarian family hierarchy. They had no work skills. There was no work. What was normality?

The very rich returned confident that the future meant rapid repossession of their expropriated shopping centres, land, industries and houses and a return to business as usual. Like the humbler migrants living in various parts of USA, they thought only in terms of the Nicaragua they had known, left, remembered and longed for. It was a rude shock for both groups to return and to find everything had changed. They had been away for ten or fifteen years. Nicaragua had moved on without them. For them, all resident Nicaraguans were seriously tainted by communism. They were told: their money was welcome but they were not wanted; they had tunnel vision; their wider experience gained in one country alone was inappropriate for the new Nicaragua; they did not know their own country. Returnees became disoriented and angry.

Resident Nicaraguans of whatever social class and whatever political persuasion had no intention of allowing the emigrants to return home and take over on their terms. Everyone who had stayed had learned a great deal about risk, danger, survival, values, propaganda, human nature, power, compromise, political ideologies and economics. Left, centrist or right wing, they had all experienced the huge effort required to achieve social and political change. Resident Nicaraguans had learned a great deal. Their convictions were hard-won and based in experience. They knew the difference between theory and praxis. They knew all about the limits of power and abuse of power. They had learned how complex and slow is the shift from policy to strategy to implementation. They used a nuanced and precise vocabulary which had resonance for all who had lived through the civil war.

Resident Nicaraguans knew what had been achieved in their country and, at what cost. They too had achieved sophistication from exposure to foreign cultures. The world had come to them in Nicaragua: European Marxists, Christians and Christian Democrats; Polish, Czechoslovakian and East German engineers and doctors who spoke excellent Spanish, worked hard, were highly educated and trained and, had their own ideas; Cuban doctors and teachers who had been in Africa (Mozambique) before they were sent to Nicaragua and whose understandings of basic education and primary health care were based in field experience. Women and men had come, made friends, talked about home and behaved according to their European or Caribbean cultures. They communicated religious and political commitments - or lack thereof. Resident Nicaraguans had listened, watched and learned. They gained a clear understanding of their place in the history and geography of the 21st century. They were very, very sophisticated in their understandings of freedom, social change, democracy and economic development. They understood that peace meant absence of civil war but not an end to the struggle.

Resident Nicaraguans were articulate; they had moved the country from dictatorship to democracy. Freedom had been achieved. Now the evolution forwards was the next phase of the struggle for the identity of a nation: a negotiated cease-fire, a democratic assembly and, a national government where the future Nicaragua was being brokered between right, centre and left visions and ideology.

The peace Nicaraguans had longed for came with a changed environment: transparency. The tasks of day to day survival during the internal struggle had meant vigilant secrecy, mistrust of anyone unfamiliar, multiple small networks, nothing on paper and a barter economy. Nicaraguans discovered they were unprepared for the future. With the peace came the outside world; openly asking for information; asking for their ideas, their signature on documents, their commitment to printed plans and their participation in round-table discussions. Nicaraguans were in culture shock. Risk, openness and productivity targets were threats to people who routinely asked no questions and never gave out their address or family name. Openness was the future.

The future also demanded acquisition of new skills, new perspectives and, new knowledge. With "the return to normality" came investors from all over the world seeking to exploit the natural resources of Nicaragua. With the brokered cease-fire came the international commercial banks. Behind them came the development financing agencies and charitable organisations. With a recognised government came offers of development aid tied to the ideologies of other organisations. The future was tied to a global economy and indebtedness - or so it would seem. The emerging question in lateral thinking and for most in Nicaragua was *"Whose Nicaragua?"*

Finally, the peace and the panic resolved itself into an awareness that there was no common ground. Banks, charities, development agencies, churches and businesses found it was easier to construct a working vocabulary and establish common ground by using short visits abroad as in-service training. Seeing the world outside rapidly oriented Nicaraguans at all levels to the working assumptions and technologies which had come to predominate while they were cut-off from worldwide change and preoccupied with their struggle. The strategy facilitated change by allowing many to move forward beyond defensiveness. "A Nicaraguan Solution for Nicaragua" began to mean Nicaraguan resolution of the issues posed for the nation by a global economy.

By mid 1992 Nicaraguans were learning to live with complexity. Some could joke that it seemed it had been easier before the cease fire when issues were clear cut (left or right). "Peace" now meant (a) coming to terms with history; (b) preserving the gains already made in the face of challenges posed to their society and their economy as their nation entered the global economy at a strong disadvantage.

Once again, the goalposts had moved. It became necessary: (a) to learn to live with complexity and (b) to think outside the box.

SOURCE NOTES

The above data is based on my experience living in Nicaragua and working with Nicaraguans from early 1990 to July 1992. I spent two weeks of every five in Nicaragua and travelled widely there in connection with my work while resident in USA.

My sources of observation are: earning my living working to U.S. strategies, serving a Roman Catholic organisation, regular plane travel between USA and Nicaragua over an 18-month period, learning the cultures and vocabularies, newspapers, T.V. and radio stations, hotels, implementing vocational and technical skills training for young guerrilla of both left and right in several locations, working alongside ordinary individuals formed by their civil war experience, initiating change, learning the limits, trust-building and listening, reflecting, adjusting to the extremely rapid pace of change.

Part III

RECONCILIATION IN ECUMENISM AND INTERFAITH RELATIONS

RECONCILIATION, *MISSIO DEI* AND THE CHURCH'S MISSION

Jacques Matthey

I - Introductory remarks

If I had to summarise in one sentence the importance of the "reconciliation" terminology in the reports from recent WCC world mission conferences or mission policy documents, I would have to confess that it plays no major role. This is even more true of "healing" and the healing ministry. I concentrate my remarks mainly on the official conference texts and documents, which can be considered to provide an image of the status of discussion among WCC member churches and affiliated mission or church councils. The observation I just made seems confirmed by the fact that "reconciliation" does not appear as a central term in David Bosch's monumental missiological masterpiece *Transforming Mission* and does not figure among the terms characterising the new ecumenical missionary paradigm. All I have said here seems particularly true of what I would call the "classical period of ecumenical missionary thinking and practice", reaching from 1952 (the world mission conference at Willingen, Germany) to 1989, the fall of the Berlin wall. It is also the period of the second major contribution of the World Council of Churches (WCC) to the ecumenical movement and church life in general, the emphasis on the struggle for justice and liberation, based on a recognition of the dignity of the poor and victims of sin[1]. The period from 1952 - 89 bears a particular theological signature, which is the reference to *missio Dei*, God's own mission, as the foundation and matrix of world mission[2].

The "reconciliation" terminology found however a place in WCC mission thinking towards the end of the eighties and the early nineties, in parallel to the renewed importance of "reconciliation" at the Canberra assembly of the WCC, held in 1991.

II - *Missio Dei* and reconciliation in ecumenical missiology, 1952 - 1989

Reconciliation was not absent from WCC mission conferences and documents, but was not highlighted in particular. My intention is to combine an evaluation of the *missio Dei* approach to witness with the appearance of the reconciliation terminology in WCC missiology. My appreciation on *missio Dei* summarises in a personal way some of the results reached at a missiological consultation organised in August 2002 in Willingen, Germany, for the 50th anniversary of the famous conference of the International Missionary Council (IMC)[3].

---

1 The first major period of the institutional existence of the WCC can be characterised by the move towards unity. From 1961 on, questions of justice and liberation became predominant. The affirmation that "reconciliation" plays no major role or no core function should not be misunderstood to mean that it doesn't appear at all. It is referred to several times in documents between 1952 and 1989. To mention but one example: in the report from section II (the kingdom of God and human struggles) of the 1980 Melbourne conference, "reconciliation" is related to the witness of churches to the demands of the gospel, pointing to forgiveness and the love of enemy, out of their participation in human struggles. It is not possible here to provide a detailed analysis of the appearance of the reconciliation language in the mission conferences.

2 The reference to *missio Dei* was not constant during the period. Around the world mission conference in Melbourne, 1980, reflection on world mission was based mainly on a theology of the kingdom of God. This explains also why *missio Dei* does not appear often in the 1982 Ecumenical Affirmation on Mission and Evangelism, whose text had been heavily influenced by the results of Melbourne.

3 The papers of the anniversary meeting in Willingen have been published in *International Review of Mission* Vol. XCII No. 367, October 2003, in parallel with a German version published by the Evangelisches Missionswerk in Hamburg (EMW). The author of this paper was the reflector at the Willingen missiological consultation. The considerations which follow are based on the reflections shared at the end of the consultation, but revisited in view of their meaning for the theme of reconciliation.

It may be important to remind ourselves of the intimate link, at Willingen itself, between the reference to God's mission and reconciliation.

"The missionary movement of which we are part has its source in the Triune God himself. Out of the depths of His love for us, the Father has sent forth His own son to reconcile all things to Himself, that we and all men might through the Spirit, be made one in Him with the Father in that perfect love which is the very nature of God."[4]

First, looking back at the beginnings of a reference to God's own dynamism, activity and purpose as the ground and horizon of our own mission, it appears to have been a liberating insight to speak of God's mission in a time of profound crisis of the missionary enterprise. In such a situation of total insecurity about the future of mission (1952), the reference to *missio Dei* took away from human shoulders the ultimate responsibility for the success or failure of Christian witness in the world. Last year we recognised to be somewhat in a similar uncertainty, living in a liminal time at the end of a period (the Christendom era) and not knowing to what future status recent developments in the economic, political or religious realms will lead the churches. The reference to *missio Dei* still makes sense in our time of crisis and the disappearance of many certainties. Despite my own personal serious reservations about the use of *missio Dei* as overall reference for missiological thinking in post-modern times[5], I accepted the positive evaluation reached at the consultation.

The second important contribution of *missio Dei* theology has been the necessary widening of the scope and content of mission over against the ecclesiocentric approach of the IMC in the post-Tambaram period. Such a "holistic" emphasis not only influenced WCC and Roman Catholic mission thinking, but also later evangelical and Pentecostal missiologists. The reference to a world-wide purpose, presence and activity of God provided the

4 "A statement on the missionary calling of the church", in: *Minutes of the enlarged meeting and the committee of the International Missionary Council, Willingen, Germany, July 5th to 21st, 1952*, London & New York, IMC, 1952, p. 54.

5 I expressed my reservations in a paper presented at the annual meeting of the German Association of Mission Studies (Deutsche Gesellschaft für Missionswissenschaft), in 2001: cf. "Mission als anstössiges Wesensmerkmal der Kirche" in: *Zeitschrift für Mission* 3/2002, pp.221-239.

basis for integrating questions related to development, liberation, dialogue with other religions, into the mission mandate and enabled a generally positive appreciation of history. In the conciliar version of *missio Dei*, the term reconciliation was however much less frequently used than "shalom", fullness of life (or "life" as such) and unity of humankind and creation.

Mission gained however such a wide meaning that it risked having any critical significance, and recently the question came up whether *missio Dei* itself had not become a meaningless umbrella term. At Willingen last year, the question was raised, whether one should not now proceed towards a more precise definition of "mission" within the wide mandate of the church.[6]

The third remark about an evaluation of *missio Dei* is somewhat more critical.

In the sixties and in particular in the West, the *missio Dei* theology provided a mainly positive appreciation of secularisation, favouring a non-religious approach to humans and societies combined with rather critical notes on the significance and role of the church. As one of the consequences, evangelism disappeared practically from the mission agenda of mainline churches in the West and North. One of the negative inheritances of the conciliar version of *missio Dei* theology is the difficulty of people of my generation to overcome the cherished ideal of the adult human being expressing his/her faith in secular terms and involvements, a typical expression of modernity[7].

Intimately linking a specific kind of analysis of society and history with the understanding of God's presence, action and intervention in the world, ecumenical missiology enabled an undeniable empowerment and strong motivation in the struggles for liberation, mainly in the South, but also in the student

---

6 cf. Tormod Engelsviken: "*Missio Dei* - Understanding and Misunderstanding of a Theological Concept in European Churches and Missiology", in *IRM*, Vol. XCII, No. 367 Oct. 2003.
The question could also be raised concerning "reconciliation". The increased use of the terminology may leave the impression that the new wine of "reconciliation" is put into the old skins of traditional ecumenical or evangelical (or Roman Catholic) mission theology.

7 This is particularly true of the reports on the study process on the "missionary structure of the congregation" in Europe and North America. The West European working group had coined the famous and very controversial expression that the world sets the agenda.

movements in the North. It however also gave rise to a political messianism which in my opinion is one of the seedbeds of violence. Whenever you link religious emotions and motivations with political interests and movements (whether ideologically situated on the left or on the right side of the spectrum), you get an explosive mixture. It is no wonder that in the 70s and 80s, many people struggled with "reconciliation", because of the difficulty to link this term with the liberation struggle and with conflict[8].

In 1989, the report of San Antonio's section II is an example of what I mean by ecumenical messianic political theology. In §4 ff, it correctly reminds that "justice" biblically speaking is more than distributive or retributive justice, but implies the building of community, with people, with God and with creation. Then however, section II affirms that the creative power of resurrection manifests itself directly when people stand up against the oppressive order of things. That may happen, says the text, through non-violent direct actions, armed rising against injustice, if all means of non-violent resistance have been tried and crushed, or through other means of confrontation as context requires. In that text, reconciliation is opposed to appeasement, because appeasement loses the creative power of the gospel, whereas reconciliation is based on the struggle, suffering, justice and even conflict.[9]

That section clearly distances itself from the earlier reflections on the power of vulnerability and non-violence (Melbourne). In San Antonio's section II report, reconciliation is associated with and not an alternative to violence. Resurrection is put in relation with people's struggles and that without any critical distance.

I come now to my fourth remark: The conciliar version of *missio Dei*, widening the understanding of mission and, even more, somewhat uncritically blending political analyses with theological messianic language, sharpened the conflict between the evangelical and ecumenical mission movements. This was one of the reasons which led to the creation in 1974 of the Lausanne Committee for World Evangelisation (LCWE) whose focus was a critique of the

---

8 The most typical example of that was of course the various versions of the Kairos document in South Africa, which e.g. David Bosch did not sign because it did not renounce violence as a last resort.

9 cf. Frederick R. Wilson (ed.): *The San Antonio report. Your Will Be Done: Mission in Christ's Way*. Geneva, WCC, 1989, pp. 39-40.

WCC and, as evangelicals said, its unilateral emphasis on political and social action, neglecting the essential task of world evangelisation and reaching the unreached. The Covenant adopted at the world consultation organised in Lausanne, Switzerland, in 1974, directly or indirectly criticises the texts from the WCC, in particular its Bangkok world mission conference 1972. We had reached the maximum point of divergence. "Although reconciliation with other people is not reconciliation with God, nor is social action evangelism, nor is political liberation salvation, nevertheless we affirm that evangelism and socio-political involvement are both part of our Christian duty."[10]

Interestingly enough, the same Covenant, and in particular the quoted paragraph, provided the basis of future less polemical encounters with evangelicals, in particular from the two thirds world. A similar assessment can be made about *missio Dei*: its extreme developments provoked and fuelled the division between churches and mission movements. In more recent times, however, its umbrella function allowed some renewed dialogues.

I now accept the case for keeping the reference to *missio Dei*, but under the condition that it be de-linked from particularist (or universalist) political theories and social analyses. If we want to build a culture of peaceful and non-violent dealing with each other, be it in the church, if we want to move towards mutual recognition, it is an urgent task to disclaim any absolute allegiance to political, ethnic or identity movements. This is not possible as long as such allegiances benefit from theological justification. To break the logic of violence – a clearly indicated aim of the Decade to Overcome Violence launched by the WCC – we missiologists must do our homework and be sure to keep a critical distance between the kingdom of God and our mission involvements, or between God's reconciling work (*missio Dei*) and our efforts towards reconciliation.

III - *Missio Dei* and reconciliation – 1989 ff

1. As already mentioned, one can discern a shift in the language used by WCC mission documents published in the nineties. The first example is taken from the report from section II of the world

10 Lausanne Covenant, §5, published in John Stott (ed.): *Making Christ known. Historic Mission Documents from the Lausanne movement, 1974-1989*, Grand Rapids, MI, Eerdmans, 1996, p. 24 (text) and 26 (Stott's commentary).

mission conference held in Salvador de Bahía, Brazil, 1996. It affirms that "The gospel reconciles and unites people of all identities into a new community where the primary and ultimate identity is identity in Jesus Christ".[11] This clear and forceful statement made in reference to Gal. 3:28 confirms a shift in the WCC's interpretation of the role of culture, ethnicity and identity. It revisits the 1972 Bangkok conference where – in a different historical context – it had been necessary to claim the right to one's identity when affirming and practising one's faith in Christ. In God's mission, human and cultural identities receive recognition as part of the richness of creation and as expression of God's gifts. That was the message in particular after Bangkok. In 1996, however, after the horrors of Rwanda and ex-Yugoslavia, and in view of the increasing tendencies to fragmentation accompanied by violence, that affirmation had to be balanced with the gospel's insistence that an identity must not be built upon the exclusion or refusal of other identities. That of course could be found in earlier WCC documents. The ethos in the ecumenical movement and the usual content of discussions often, however, still insisted mainly on the right to one's identity, without the qualifying addition. Since Salvador, to receive reconciliation and participate in Christ's body means to affirm one's cultural identity as an open one, ready to dialogue with other identities and to be enriched through relations.

In the late eighties and in the nineties, WCC documents put much more emphasis on the link between a reference to *missio Dei* and the use of reconciliation and unity to express its content. Biblical references shift now to the letter to the Ephesians[12]: "A

11 see Christopher Duraisingh (ed.): *Called to One Hope. The Gospel in Diverse Cultures.* Geneva, WCC, 1998, p. 46.

12 In particular the hymns of Ephesians 1 and 2.During the "classical" period of ecumenical missiology, there was a preferred reference to the gospels, in particular the three synoptic gospels, and the book of Acts. Luke 4: 16 ff (gospel for the poor) or John 10:10 (fullness of life) as well as Matthew 25:31-45 (Christ present among the poor) were favourite texts. Paul, and in particular his recognised classical letters, was not a key reference. This may explain in part why after 1961, reconciliation was not highlighted so much in WCC mission documents. Thematically speaking, during the sixties and seventies, the words and acts of Jesus as described by the gospels played an important role as "model" for discipleship. Christ, the one dying on the cross for the redemption of humankind, would appear in liturgical confessional expressions only. From the middle 70s on, the challenge to link witness and solidarity in affirmations on mission found its best expression in a theology of the kingdom of God.

reconciled humanity and renewed creation is the goal of the mission of the church. The vision of God uniting all things in Christ is the driving force of its life and sharing"[13]. In the preparatory document for the 1996 conference, Christopher Duraisingh wrote in reference to II Cor. 5 that God took the initiative to reconcile the world to Godself, and that, having received that gift, the church is called to be a sign and foretaste of what humanity is to become. The purpose of mission is to build communities that can live in communion with God and one another, resisting the increasingly divisive forces active in the world[14].

It seems clear that since 1989, *missio Dei* reappears forcefully in WCC missiology, linked again, as had been the case at Willingen, with "reconciliation". This renewed emphasis makes sense, as already mentioned, but under certain conditions, which were discussed at the anniversary consultation in 2002.

2. A renewed reference to *missio Dei* in the beginning of the 21st century needs to take into account the increasing difficulty to discern causes and consequences of developments in societies shaken by violence and war. The complexity of events and trends and the reaction against world-explaining grand narratives must be taken seriously[15]. How can we say we know what God's purposes are in history, when whole generations of people are swept away

---

13 The sentence appears in the report from section III ("Spirit of Unity – Reconcile your people") from the WCC Canberra assembly. Cf. Michael Kinnamon (ed.): *Signs of the Spirit. Official report, WCC Seventh Assembly*. Geneva, WCC and Grand Rapids, Eerdmans, 1991, p. 100. The sentence, taken from the chapter B, "Mission in the power of the Spirit – the ministry of reconciliation and sharing", is quoted or referred to in all-important WCC mission documents since Canberra.

14 The preparatory document for Salvador, drafted by Christopher Duraisingh, then executive secretary for Gospel and Cultures in WCCs Unit II "Churches in Mission: Health, Education, Witness", contains all important matters dealt with at the world mission conference of 1996, in most cases better formulated than the official section reports of the conference itself. To understand the vision behind the study process on gospel and cultures in the WCC, one should refer to the preparatory document and to the papers written by Duraisingh in the official book.

15 Bert Hoedemaker made clear in many papers how much *missio Dei* and the whole ecumenical movement could be considered typical products of the age of modernity, seriously challenged in the end of the 20th century with the move to postmodernity. As examples one can refer to: Bert Hoedemaker: *Secularization and Mission. A Theological Essay*. Harrisburg, PA, Trinity Press International, 1998, Christian Mission and Modern Culture series, 82p., in particular pp. 31ff. One of the shortest and clearest presentations of Hoedemaker's point of view can be found in: *Id.*: "Mission, Unity and Eschaton". In: *Reformed World* Vol. 50, No. 4, Dec. 2000, pp. 173-182.

by a pandemic such as HIV/AIDS? We have not yet taken seriously enough in ecumenical missiology that we may well live in a time in which it is impossible to make overall affirmations about God and world developments trends.

However, as was said in Willingen last year, even in such a context of increasing ambiguity it makes sense to continue to use *missio Dei*. I would personally plead for referring to it as a metaphor for God's love and presence, God's unconditional accessibility (which is what the reconciliation message of the gospel conveys). However, we must take care of linking this part of the biblical message with another, less comforting and not at all politically correct in ecumenical circles: we must never lose sight of affirming in the same way God's unavailability, God's unknown and perhaps even disturbing if not frightening aspects, which may include judgement in ways we do not like or expect. That the Bible has to speak of "reconciliation" implies indeed that there is enmity between God and humanity. To speak of "reconciliation" as the core of *missio Dei* edifies and comforts, but also shakes and challenges.

3. To nurture the vision of reconciliation, unity in diversity – for church and humankind – ecumenical missiologists refer to the trinitarian dimension of *missio Dei*, to the intimate link between the three persons of the Trinity. In recent texts of Faith and Order, Mission and Evangelism as well as the recent Willingen consultation, there is an insistence that we must not separate the Father from the Son and the Spirit. This has several consequences for missiology. Two may be hinted at here: it means first that we cannot limit the scope of Christ or of the Spirit to inner-church circles and affairs. This confirms the wide interpretation of mission since 1952. The second consequence, however, is that such an approach does not allow us to speak of the Spirit's presence in the world without maintaining the Spirit's close relationship with Christ. That may challenge some versions of pluralist theologies of religions. My hope is that we can keep this coherence while giving space to the specificity and freedom of each person of the Trinity and so remain fundamentally open to receive any unforeseen revelatory, healing or reconciling dynamics of the Spirit.

I would however personally hesitate to allow for any more precise description of inner-trinitarian *processiones*, as was often attempted in past and present times. Who are we to know the inner life of God? Some theologies seem to fall into the temptation of transferring to God politically correct and relevant visions of the ideal community, church or society. We are called to *interpret* the clearest image we received of the reconciling God, i.e. Jesus Christ, and to *discern* God's presence, activity, dynamics through the Spirit wherever the Spirit touches us. But to interpret and to discern may not be the same as to explain and build a system. I would like us to stick to an "apophatic" *missio Dei* theology. Ecumenical missiology, whether written in the North or the South, is still too much oriented by a Western world-view and understanding of history.

4. Eventually the need has arisen to recapture the importance and role of the church in ecumenical missiology. In its conciliar version, *missio Dei* has become the missionary paradigm par excellence that does not attribute an important role to the church. The request for renewed missional ecclesiology has come up as a counter-point to some extreme versions of ecumenical missiology. It has now been heard within ecumenical as well as evangelical circles, and is needed to prevent extreme approaches to mission from a socio-political or managerial-pragmatic side[16].

---

16 WCC texts show a remarkable consistency in their emphasis on unity whenever the reconciliation terminology comes up, even during the decades of the most radical *missio Dei* approach in missiology. It must be said that there has always been a balance between more political and more ecclesial emphases in WCC mission conferences, the former usually getting more public and media attention. It is interesting to read the texts of all sections of two of the most politicised world mission conferences to understand that there has never been a real neglect of the church's specific calling in ecumenical mission documents. Cf. Bangkok's section III (Churches renewed in mission) and Melbourne's section III (The Church witnesses to the kingdom) as well as the sections I and IV of San Antonio. The same must be said of the 1982 Affirmation on Mission and Evangelism. It remains true, however, that the ethos and programmatic priorities of WCC mission discourse and practice did not always sufficiently mirror the balance found in the texts. In recent years, the shift towards a renewed ecclesiology is evident. Ecclesiological emphases appear in the study document "Mission and Evangelism in Unity Today" of the years 1998 - 2000. The most recent Faith and Order (F&O) study paper on ecclesiology has remarkable missiological accents (*The Nature and Purpose of the Church. A stage on the way to a common statement.* Geneva, WCC, 1998, 61 p. Faith and Order paper No. 181). The shift led to the organisation of a common consultation between the F&O Commission and the Commission on World Mission and Evangelism (CWME) precisely on ecclesiology and mission, which has been documented in: *IRM* Vol. XC, No. 358, July 2001. Ecclesiology also appears important in the recent mission statement coming out of the Iguassu consultation organised by the missions commission of the World Evangelical Fellowship (1999) as well as in its ongoing study work (William D.

A renewed *missio Dei* theology must find a balance between God's overall activity and presence in the world and God's presence and action through Christian communities. This requests a renewed appreciation of worship (including eucharist), spirituality but also of evangelism, within ecumenical missiology. A really holistic understanding of mission includes a commitment to the proclamation of the gospel. "Evangelism aims to build up a reconciling and reconciled community (cf. 2 Cor. 5:19) that will point to the fullness of God's reign, which is 'righteousness and peace and joy in the Holy Spirit' (Rom. 14:17)". This affirmation of the preparatory document for Salvador finds an echo in the recent WCC mission statement: "To speak of evangelism means to emphasise the proclamation of God's offer of freedom and reconciliation, together with the invitation to join those who follow Christ and work for the reign of God."[17].

This is the tradition on which the CWME has built the most recent proposals of a thematic emphasis of mission for the coming world mission conference.

But before turning to that, I intend to comment from my personal point of view on some missiological consequences of the way Paul uses the "reconciliation " terminology in the letters which are clearly attributed to him, i.e. II Corinthians and Romans.

IV - Reconciliation in Paul's letters

Particularly because reconciliation seems such a well-adapted terminology for a renewed perspective on mission in the beginning of the 21st century, we must take seriously the fact that the "reconciliation" terminology is rare in the Bible. It is practically non-existent in the First Testament, and in the New Testament, it

---

Taylor, ed.: *Global Missiology for the 21st Century. The Iguassu Dialogue*. Grand Rapids, MI, and World Evangelical Fellowship, 2000, 564 pp.). There is no need to emphasise that Roman Catholic and Orthodox missiologies had always kept the intimate link with the role of the church.

17 The first sentence is taken from: *CWME Salvador, Bahia, Brazil, 24 November – 3 December 1996, Preparatory Papers for Section Work*, Geneva, WCC Unit II, 1996, p. 19.
The second sentence is quoted from "Mission and Evangelism in Unity Today", § 62. Printed in: *IRM* Vol. LXXXVIII Nos. 348/49, Jan/April 1999, pp. 109-127. That document, prepared by the WCC's Unit II (Churches in Mission: Health, Education, Witness) had been discussed in a workshop of the Harare assembly of the WCC and was later submitted to the new WCC Commission on World Mission and Evangelism which adopted it as a study document at its meeting in 2000.

appears practically only in the Pauline literature and even there not very often. I interpret this is a sign that we should use "reconciliation" only with discernment. I will concentrate my remarks on certain aspects of the use of "reconciliation" in the letters for which Paul is clearly identified as the author[18].

II Corinthians

1. I asked myself why, in II Corinthians 5, Paul describes the renewed relation between God and humans with a term he never used before. "Reconciliation" appears in the relatively peaceful and calm description he gives of the apostolic ministry, enabled by and according to the Spirit (II Cor. 3-6). I would like to submit the following hypothesis: these chapters of II Cor. seem to have been written following a very painful experience Paul made of a very serious attack not only on his ministry and authority, but on him as a person. The incident on which we do not know much occurred during one of the visits of Paul or of one of his team members to Corinth[19] and jeopardised the whole relations between the apostolic mission team and that community. Paul felt the need to write a stern rebuke to the whole church, asking for clear measures of discipline to be taken against that man. Only such measures would prove that the community distances itself from the injury. The Corinthians accepted to start a procedure against the offender. This restoration of confidence between the church and the apostles brought Paul back to a more friendly tone: "This punishment by the majority is enough for such a person; so now instead you should forgive and console him, so that he may not be overwhelmed by excessive sorrow. So I urge you to reaffirm your love for him" (II Cor. 2:6-8, NRSV).

It makes sense to interpret Paul's experience as a possible reason why in chapters 3-5, Paul can not only present his

18 Other central aspects of "reconciliation" in the Pauline literature are well dealt with in other papers presented at this BIAMS consultation and there is no need to repeat them. Cf. in particular Robert Schreiter's contributions.

19 The incident is mentioned in II Cor. 2: 1ff. There is uncertainty among biblical scholars as to what exactly happened. Some exegetes think that the personal attack on Paul took place during a visit made by a member of his mission team, perhaps Timotheus. Others opt for the possibility of an interim visit of Paul himself to Corinth, one not mentioned in Acts, a visit interrupted because of the incident. The text II Cor. 2:1 leaves both interpretations open. The various hypotheses are linked to the choice about how many letters Paul may have written to the community in Corinth. For the purpose of the argumentation in this paper, it suffices to refer to the seriousness of the incident, touching Paul very profoundly.

apostolate in a calm and systematic way, but also reinterprets the event of Christ's death in terms of "reconciliation" between God and humankind, as expression of God's love and forgiveness[20].

In the famous passage of II Cor 5, reconciliation describes the significance of Christ's death "for us" on the cross, that central part of some of the earliest confessions of faith. In Paul's letters, Christ is not first and foremost an ethical model. In and through him, God offers salvation and peace to each of us, humans, putting an end to enmity. In Paul's theology, the dramatic breakdown of relations between God and humanity (called "sin") is of such amplitude that reconciliation, the reestablishment of peace, is nothing less than the beginning of the eschatological "new creation".

2. What is the "ministry of reconciliation" in II Cor. 5? The apostolic task of Paul and his team, characterising the apostolic ministry of the church in general, is to call humans – within and without the church – to accept reconciliation. Men and women are taken seriously as responsible creatures and thus are called to accept and receive the paradigm change made possible for them by God in Christ. To become effective in the present time or, to say it differently, to become part of human experience, God's reconciling act needs a human response and is consequently embedded in an evangelistic message. The ministry of reconciliation entrusted to the church is to proclaim what God has done in Christ and to call us to accept reconciliation. Directly or indirectly, this is to realise that, without accepting God's offer, we might not be in right relations with God. It may seem strange in post-modern times, but the "reconciliation" terminology of the NT implies that there is "sin" or separation from God. If there is no grave offence or even enmity, it makes no sense to speak of reconciliation.

3. To describe the activity I have now - not without a slightly polemical note - called "evangelism", Paul uses the Greek term "parakalein", which means: ask for help; exhort; console or give

20 The term "reconciliation", rare, but existing in the Jewish tradition also had a political meaning for the Corinthians. If however that was the main point of reference for Paul and the community, the question remains why he did not make use of it in his earlier correspondence with the community, in particular when dealing with the divisions and conflicting groups (I Cor. 1:10 ff and the argumentation on the basis of Christ's death on the cross).

consoling help[21] "parakalein" is used for communication ad intra and ad extra. Unlike the modern term "evangelism" it has no aggressive undertone, and combines the seriousness of the appeal in reference to God's salvation with the character of a pressing invitation, the call to live in accordance with one's faith, but also the pastorally consoling helpful word between people who walk together on the way of Christian life. The verb and the noun are used in the NT and in particular in Pauline literature to summarise the missionary activity altogether. To be able to exhort and console in this way is also considered by Paul one of the charisms of the Spirit and a major expression of the prophetic ministry of the church[22].

Often, Paul indicates the main items of his message in the first paragraphs of a letter, after the traditional greeting. It seems important to note that the "parakalein" terminology appears ten times in verses 3-7 of the first chapter of II Corinthians. Its use is constant throughout the letter. One could even say that it appears that the correspondence between Paul and the church in Corinth is an example of such a pastoral mission[23]. The term comes to describe God's identity as the one who consoles the downcast, the small, humble, unimportant ones (II Cor. 7:6), the "God of all consolation" (II Cor. 1:3, NRSV). It seems fair to speak of God's preferential option for the victims[24].

---

21 cf. Gerhard Friedrich (ed.): *Theological Dictionary of the New Testament,* Vol. V. Grand Rapids, MI, Eerdmans, 1967, pp. 793-799. My use of "evangelism" is not exactly correct, since the NT term euangelizesthai doesn't appear. Usually that verb is used exclusively for Jesus' and/or the first apostles' preaching and healing activity. In the gospels it is linked to the good news announced to the poor, in the epistles, it describes the opening official announcement of the breaking in of the "last times" with the establishment of Christ as Kyrios. In this paper, I use the term "evangelism" in a contemporary meaning as it appears in the recent WCC mission documents, stressing the sharing of the good news combined with an invitation to consider to link one's life with Christ and the gospel message. Cf. "Mission and Evangelism in Unity", *op. cit. IRM*.

22 cf. Rom. 12:8 and I Cor. 14:3, 31.

23 Paul also uses the verb parakalein when asking the church to speak an exhorting and/or consoling word to the man who offended him so seriously (II Cor. 2:7,..forgive and *console* him.....).

24 In reference to the famous formulation of "God's preferential option for the poor" in the documents from the meeting of the bishops of Latin America (CELAM) in Medellin 1968. One should however always remember that God's options cannot be systematised in exclusive ways. We should refrain from giving to the "victims" today the role messianic theology attributed to the "poor" or the "damned of the earth" in recent decades. Such affirmations should provide critical criteria to judge

I usually do not switch from one NT writer to another, but I cannot at this stage refrain from the remark that John uses "parakletos" to qualify the Spirit and the Spirit's mission[25].

4. I find it extremely important to underline that in II Cor. reconciliation is first and foremost part of God's own mission only (*Missio Dei*). The church's apostolic ministry in reference to reconciliation is evangelistic or pastoral. I wouldn't like to separate these terms in the present discussion, because the one corrects the other. If I only use evangelism, there is a risk that I am understood as favouring aggressive evangelistic campaigns, which I do not. Paul himself struggles against evangelistic crusaders in II Cor. 12-14. If I only use "pastoral" I could give the impression to justify whatever is (not) done as expression of the pastoral ministry in our churches, most of the times not really mission-focused. Keeping both terms in tension qualifies the ministry of reconciliation as one expressing God's love and grace without emptying it of the urgency of a communication requesting an answer.

I plead for mission to recover the Christian message about God as its main content and *raison d'être*. It seems fair to say that because of recent developments in the world of religious life and particularly in post-modern contexts, this specifically religious task of mission must be stressed much more than is usually done in ecumenical discussions. The ministry of reconciliation is first a word about what God offers, and an urgent word indeed: "Now is the time!" (II Cor. 6:2). I would not hesitate to say that without us daring to share the gospel in such a pastorally sensitive way, other parts of our ministry fail to reflect Paul's understanding of reconciliation.

Romans

1. When writing to the Romans, Paul again uses "reconciliation" to describe the establishment of peace by God, in strict parallelism with his preferred "justification" terminology. At the core of one of the key passages of the whole letter, 5:1-11, he

---

missionary theologies and practices rather than building blocks for a theology of history.

25 There is a certain parallel in the sense that Paul himself qualifies his apostolic ministry in II Cor 3-5 as the ministry of the new covenant, marked by the Spirit. However, the Johannine use of "parakletos" has its specific meaning which cannot be dealt with in this paper.

puts a particular emphasis on the way the Spirit allows the believer to experience emotionally and intellectually Christ's act of love on the cross: "Such a hope is no mockery, because God's love has flooded our inmost heart through the Holy Spirit he has given us" (Rom. 5:5, New English Bible). The passage has a charismatic touch. It shows that reconciliation and peace with God are real for us when we have been filled by the Spirit and so fully renewed in the innermost core and centre of our being. A spirituality of reconciliation grows on such a fundamental identity-building experience of renewed persons.

2. But the letter to the church living in the capital of the empire draws larger implications of the reconciling act of God in Christ than II Cor. Romans can be read as a theological meditation on the significance of history for human groups and societies, as a "peace memorandum"[26]. The overall composition of Romans shows that the reconciliation given in Christ intrinsically links the "vertical" and "horizontal" elements of peace. Romans builds on God's refusal to make any qualitative difference between humans according to their cultural or religious origin (Rom. 2:11). Human groups have all the same value before God: *all* are sinners, Jews as well as Gentiles, *all* have access to God through their traditions and experience (but somewhat make a wrong use of it), Christ died for *all*, *all* are called to accept that fact, *all* can receive access to God, independently of their religious affiliation and cultural identity, and Paul expresses the hope that *all* may be saved. Theologically speaking, the existing Christian groups in Rome and in the empire, formed by people of Jewish and Gentile origins, represent symbolically all possible existing and future human ethnic, religious, social or national groupings[27].

Based on his understanding of "reconciliation" as establishment of peace, Paul develops something like a "meta-narrative" of global history as moving towards an end with a positive outcome for all human groups (including creation) in chapters 8-11. Despite Paul's radical critical tone, he seems to envisage re-

---

26 I found the term "peace memorandum" in: Klaus Haacker: "Der Römerbrief als Friedensmemorandum", *New Testament Studies* Vol., 36, 1990, pp. 25-41.

27 Whether there were different groups in one church or different churches in Rome does not change fundamentally the question. It is also more than plausible to suppose that Paul knew his letter would be circulated in the whole of the empire.

established right relations between God and the "fullness" of Jews as well as the "fullness" of the nations at the very end of history[28].

3. "May the God of steadfastness and encouragement (paraklesis) grant you to live in harmony with one another, in accordance with Christ Jesus, so that together you may with one voice glorify the God and Father of our Lord Jesus Christ. Welcome one another, therefore, just as Christ has welcomed you, for the glory of God." (15:6-7, NRSV)

I want to stress three main aspects of mission according to Romans. They must shape the church's response to God's reconciliation.

(A) Group or individual boasting, closed and exclusive identity, group or individual superiority complexes have to be overcome. They are characteristic of what Paul calls life "under the Law"[29]. To this Paul opposes life under God's grace, of which faith as humble acceptance of God's reconciliation, is the expression. The tragedy of Christian mission is to have transformed Paul's vision into its opposite, by creating new closed identity systems around a narrow understanding of faith or ethics, often linked to the Christendom paradigm. We have again created systems of "just" and "unjust" on the basis of human achievements, whether in the form of right, correct dogmatic faith, or of right morality, or of fully developed church disciplines, absolute church constitutions or canonical laws. These systems have been used – and still are – to create or maintain divisions between groups and churches, thus

28 "For if their (my own people's) rejection is the reconciliation of the world, what will their acceptance be but life from the dead" (11:15). It should be noted that Paul's approach is one of vision and hope. He does not pretend to know the future (11:33ff) and in that sense, does not develop a theology of history. He uses the term "pleroma" in parallel for Jews and for Gentiles. One must not interpret the one differently from the other. Depending on the way one relates these affirmations with other ones in Paul's letters, the "fullness" has a qualitative or quantitative character. There always remains an unresolved tension in Paul's literature between an exclusive and a universal trend. In any case, it seems that the multicultural composition of the church reflects the multicultural quality and composition of the eschatological vision. The exhortation in Rom. 12 – 15 to live according to that future gives to the epistle to the Romans its coherent character.

29 This should not be understood as in any way a historical judgement. I am not pretending here that Judaism, whether historical or present, bears more characteristics of such life "under the law" as any other religion, including Christianity. Recent exegetical research has shown how much more subtle Paul's relations with the various schools of Judaism were in his time than traditional Protestant biblical work had pretended.

jeopardising the witness Paul requested of the Romans. Where does our proclamation of God's gracious offer remain, when we cannot express unity because of such human legal systems? If churches offer their services to the "world" on behalf of their competence in reconciliation, they also must show the world that their spirituality allows them to overcome denominational as well as other divisions[30]. It's a question of credibility.

I need to add a footnote. It would be misunderstanding Paul's message, if one pushes the texts to only affirm universal salvation. There remains in Paul as well in the whole of the NT a tension between exclusivist affirmations about salvation through faith in Christ and a universalist perspective of salvation or union of all in God under Christ. It is not my intention here to offer a solution to that dilemma for the interpreter. I want however to stress that whatever position one chooses to consider, it must not lead to new forms of group superiority complex. Churches or theologians who force the NT testimonies in one or the other direction may well contribute to the formation of spiritual blocks and so in some way work against one of the major intentions of Paul.

(B) The church's mission is to build communities where people can find a healing home, a place to tell their story, to experience and share love and understanding, a pastoral accompaniment (parakalein) but also the joy of charismatic blessings of the Lord. Such missional churches will be empowered even to bless their enemies (which is the non aggressive evangelism *par excellence*) and work for peace and good in the whole city, today we would say for justice, peace and the integrity of creation (a creation which in Romans is mysteriously in solidarity with humanity in its pains and hope)[31].

---

30 The argument is valid for any divisive frontier, whether denominational, ethnic, racial or other. In some contexts the ethnic divisions (or the racial: apartheid) are the most damaging to Christian witness, in others its the denominational. Often they are linked. In the context of increasing fragmentation, one can ask the question, whether the denominational divisions are not the most scandalous ones that churches as churches have to deal with.

31 This paragraph summarises Rom. 12 which describes in Pauline terms what we mean when we speak of a healing and reconciling community. The attitude requested in Rom. 12 and ff must be read in relation with the exhortations and challenges Paul addresses to people of Jewish and of Gentile origins in 9 – 11 particularly.

(C) Paul adds a specific consequence of reconciliation and peace in the realm of what we would call today "world mission". The collection for the Jerusalem church for which he asks support, is an offer made on behalf of the receiving churches of the Gentile world to the first sending church in Jerusalem: in the name of God, accept our gift as a sign of recognition and peace. The collection is meant to manifest concretely this mutual acceptance in the face of God by both major "denominational" groups and conflicting mission movements of the first century. There had been severe wounds in mission between Paul and his missionary school and the Jerusalem Christians. Paul had been attacked sharply and had answered just as sharply. It was not natural for him to go back with this "inter-church aid", and it was not at all natural for the strict Jewish Christians to accept such a sign. Accepting it would have meant a recognition of Paul's ministry and mission. We do not know whether it was accepted and there is serious doubt about that among scholars[32].

V - "Come Holy Spirit, heal and reconcile".
"Called in Christ to be reconciling and healing communities".

These are the title and thematic area of the coming WCC world mission conference to be held in Athens, Greece, May 12-19, 2005. I will use them to summarise what I tried to convey to you today.

Full healing and reconciliation is the purpose and result of God's mission (*missio Dei*) and God's mission only. Healing in the widest sense of the word, as well as reconciliation, is not and must not be hoped for as the expected result of human action and the church's mission. Basically, full healing and real reconciliation are "eschatological" goods, fully realised in and through Christ's life, death and resurrection, consummated at the end of times. "Eschatological" also means that full healing and reconciliation can be experienced today, but only in the presence and by

32 This is one more example of a biblical story of reconciliation which is open-ended. I would even make the hypothesis that the majority of stories or parables dealing indirectly or directly with reconciliation do not bring a final solution, but leave us with an ongoing task. This is another proof that the biblical authors stress how much reconciliation can only be God's business. Even when dealing with God, the stories may have an open end. In Luke 15, the story of the prodigal son, the question of a reconciliation between the father or the younger son and the older son/brother remains open ended and does not give us his answer. Perhaps because the message of reconciliation offered by God always requests our own answer.

the grace of God. This is what we express through our prayer to and invocation of the Holy Spirit, God's healing and reconciling *presence*. We pray that we may expect and experience real signs of that presence today, in a non-reconciled, non-healed, world and humanity. Through our prayer, we also affirm our hope that God continually sends the Spirit, to heal and reconcile. We cannot foresee where that will happen nor on behalf of whom nor for whom, but this is the ground of our hope, faith and action: the final result of *missio Dei*, not bypassing judgement, but overcoming judgement by grace, will be a new creation reconciled with God.

Within God's overall mission, the church has a central and irreplaceable role. This is formulated in the thematic area of the conference and refers to the specific calling of Christian churches to be reconciling and healing communities. Ecumenical strategy for mission in the beginning of the 21st century is to multiply communities, spaces, where people can find signs of the healing and reconciliation offered in the name of Christ and so experience how good and gracious God is. Unlike other missionary movements, the WCC has no major conquering evangelism strategy for the world or the unreached. We trust that existing or new local churches and communities, inspired and empowered by the Holy Spirit and who follow the footsteps of Jesus and the early Christians, will be attractive enough to provide a home for those who seek God, yearning for meaning, peace and protection from evil. What this exactly means is to be discerned in each specific context, and in ecumenical and intercultural dialogue or hermeneutics.

I want to conclude by indicating some of the most urgent mission contributions to reconciliation today[33]:

---

33 The emphases that follow must not be understood as exclusive ones. The overall study programme towards the world mission conference lists the following signposts which must guide us in our search for a meaningful response to the reconciliation message today: identity in a constantly changing and increasingly plural world (issues include: definition of identity in relation to other identities and identities in conflict; mission and theology of religions; multicultural ministry), healing and reconciling ministry (issues include: dialogue between different approaches, from Pentecostal/charismatic to liturgical/sacramental and multidisciplinary; HIV/AIDS as a challenge to mission); the search for alternative communities (i.e. living according to alternative values to globalisation, either economically or culturally speaking); be a missional and evangelising church (ecumenical approaches to theology and practice of evangelism). More details can be found on the specific CWME Conference pages on the WCC Website: www.wcc-coe.org

First: There has been in recent years a dangerous tendency to accept stepbacks in the search for church unity. The dynamics of fragmentation affect churches all over the world, and the increasingly open religious market pushes them not just to state their specificity, but to do so in an increasingly competitive manner, based on closed identity and the insistence on the points which separate. It's a competition over souls and money, a search for influence, power and status. The actual fragmentation jeopardises not only agreements reached in the 20th century, but the ecumenical movement as such. What is our competence in reconciliation, what is our credibility in the world of politics, social and ethnic conflicts, if we are not able to maintain those bonds of unity we have reached? Hospitality is one of the major values of community life in the NT. Common prayer is another. How can it be that we still have not been able to let that inspire the whole of our church life?

We should use all forces to turn the wheel into the direction of an alternative to globalisation by working for real church unity in diversity. In missional terms, this means to really put into practice all the excellent texts we have produced on common witness. In the ecumenical world, we are good at criticising all those doing proselytism. The basis of proselytism is the belief that one's expression of faith is the only one valid. But are the difficulties of mainline churches to co-operate in mission not rooted in the same closed understanding of identity?

Why is it so difficult to organise and plan mission in common – in whatever kind of evangelistic, diaconal, pastoral, healing or political mode - leaving everybody free to respond and join that community which best corresponds to their understanding of the gospel and their spiritual needs?

As *second* specifically missionary challenge I want to mention the increasing re-colonisation of North-South relations (North meaning economic and political or religious centres, South meaning those regions, people and churches which are peripheries in relation to these centres). The recent Iraq war is a political and military face of this re-colonisation. But the trend among donors, parishes and communities, to decide on the way their money is to be used is again on the increase, after a period of confidence in the partners during the sixties and seventies. Re-colonisation has made its way into churches, mission bodies and development agencies through extreme forms of the request for management through planning, monitoring and evaluation. This has somewhat developed into an ideology, based on a Western understanding of efficiency, time and history. Multilateral ecclesial institutions – including the WCC – are challenged as ineffective (parallel to what happens to UN institutions), church communities for mission in real partnership such as Cevaa and CWM[34] are under the pressure to modify their way of dealing with power and money. Development agencies have established their own regional offices, copying the old colonial system of the inspectorates of mission societies. These trends are a fundamental challenge to justice in North-South relations.

Paul struggled to express the dignity of both the church of Jerusalem and the churches of the Gentile people by taking great care in the way he dealt with the collection. Today, the way churches and mainly church agencies deal with their partners seldom recognises them with a really equal identity. I strongly affirm that the move towards the transformation of earlier intercontinental mission societies into church communities for mission was an attempt at starting a journey towards reconciliation between people on the sending and receiving side of organised mission. Since 1989, such steps have been increasingly undermined, despite the rhetoric on "restorative" or "transformative" justice, of which Cevaa and CWM are probably together with some ecumenical programs of the sixties, the most illuminating attempts.

The *third* major example I want to give concerns HIV/AIDS, and I draw on a paper presented at the recent meeting of the WCC Commission on World Mission and Evangelism by Christoph Benn, from the German Institute for Medical Mission. "From the beginning of the HIV/AIDS pandemic that started in 1981 there has been a deep division between many churches and people who

34 The Cevaa – Community of Churches in Mission – grew out of the fundamental restructuring of the Paris Mission in the late sixties and early seventies. It now has its headquarters in Montpellier, France. The Council for World Mission (CWM), formerly the London Missionary Society, was created out of a similar attempt to reach more justice in partnership relations. A summarised description of their importance can be found in two papers by Kai Funkschmidt: "Partnership between Unequals – Mission Impossible? Mission Structures Revisited" in: *IRM* Vol. XCI No. 362, July 2002, pp. 395-413, and "New models of Mission Relationship and Partnership" in: *IRM* Vol. XCI No. 363, October 2002, pp. 558 – 576.

became infected with HIV/AIDS. Churches very often regarded the infection as self-inflicted and related to the life style or behaviour of the infected people themselves. People suffering from this disease felt excluded from Christian congregations and communities, they were described as sinners, as practising abnormal behaviour and some were even told that their disease was the punishment of God. This situation led to a lot of discrimination, stigma and left many people traumatised by their church in times when they actually needed care, support, unconditional love and acceptance, and a safe place where they could share their story.

There have also been deep divisions between churches because of different dogmatic and ethical traditions. Churches issued various statements on HIV/AIDS sometimes contradicting each other which made co-operation more difficult.

Therefore reconciliation is needed both between the churches and with people who are suffering and are stigmatised as the lepers were in the time of Jesus. Also churches need reconciliation among themselves to be able to work together meaningfully to address one of the most serious global threats accounting for 3 million deaths per year and a major obstacle to socio-economic development and political stability in many countries and regions of our world "[35] In this realm, there is particular importance for the missional congregations to recover their call to be reconciling and healing communities, following the exhortation found in Rom. 12 (see above). HIV/AIDS however is also a test-case for a holistic understanding of and approach to mission, since almost all possible elements of human and societal life influence the development and consequences of the pandemic. Mission is incomplete if people only find a home in healing communities, but if the church and its mission or development bodies do not challenge the structural causes of the pandemic.

The *fourth* point which I want to mention is the need for a reconciliation with the evangelical and Pentecostal mission movements. In case of the evangelicals, this refers to the split radically manifested in 1961 when the IMC integrated with the WCC and more in 1974 when the Lausanne Committee for World

35 Christoph Benn: *Reconciliation between churches and people living with HIV/AIDS*. Unpublished case-study presented at the April 2003 meeting of the WCC Commission on World Mission and Evangelism, p. 1.

Evangelisation was created. In the case of Pentecostals, there is a necessary healing of memories because of the way many of them have been treated by most mainline churches, and often react in consequence. Wounds have been inflicted and received on both sides, and the question of steps towards some reconciliation will become urgent as we move towards 2010, the 100th anniversary of the famous world mission conference in Edinburgh.

There are some hopeful signs of a possible new relationship. I have mentioned some theological developments in my paper, and contacts have been established between people of good will. As one of the most fascinating examples, I want to point to the continuing dialogue between the Roman Catholic Church and Pentecostals, started in the early seventies. It produced very important documents, not least on mission theology, and led leading persons in both groups to offer words of confession of sins and of forgiveness[36].

Dialogue with Pentecostals/charismatics and evangelicals is an increasingly relevant aspect of the "North-South" debate in mission. If indeed the centre of gravity of Christianity is moving to the continents of Asia, Africa and Latin America, this bears not only geographical significance. Many of the churches and mission movements of the regions of the South are nurtured by evangelical and Pentecostal spirituality, as are most of the migrant churches in the North. Steps towards dialogue between divided mission movements will also contribute to take them seriously as partners and recognise their dignity.

The last point I want to mention today is the Decade to Overcome Violence of which the subtitle is "churches seeking reconciliation and peace"[37]. Four aspects of the culture of violence are to be addressed until 2010(!), the spirit and logic of violence; the use, abuse and misuse of power; issues of justice; religious identity and plurality. I tried to convey in the preceding reflections

---

36 An exhaustive description of the missionary importance from a Pentecostal point of view can be found in: Veli-Matti Kärkkäinen: *Ad Ultimum Terrae. Evangelization, Proselytism and Common Witness in the Roman Catholic Pentecostal Dialogue (1990-1997)*, Frankfurt/M., Peter Lang, 1999, 281 p. (Studies in the Intercultural History of Christianity No 117).
The confessions of Kilian McDonnell and Frank Macchia were also published in: *IRM* Vol. LXXXIX No. 355 with an introduction by Walter Hollenweger, pp. 568-571.

37 Visit DOV pages on the WCC Website. Cf www.wcc-coe.org

how these questions affect the mission movement and mission theology and how by working on our internal affairs, we could make a contribution to the DOV from within the experience of churches in mission. The logic of violence and the use of power have much to do with messianic influences on theology, with our understanding of group identity, with wrong emphases in trinitarian theologies, and issues of justice are central in the mentioned North-South relations and partnerships.

In **conclusion**, the preparatory process for the next world mission conference will attempt to highlight a spirituality of reconciliation[38] as perhaps the most important contribution churches in mission could bring to actual conflicts in church and world. Such a spirituality is built on three pillars:

We need *persons* profoundly, which means also emotionally, touched by God's love poured in their hearts by the Spirit. Without the active involvement of persons who experienced such reconciliation themselves, no process, be it within or without the church, can be sustained in the long term. That is why the first aim of the CWME conference of 2005, is the renewal of participants themselves, so that they can return to their specific mission encouraged and empowered.

Our mission strategy is to build and multiply *communities* which can offer a space for reconciliation and healing and through their pastoral communication of the message edify people, motivate persons that it is worth today to believe in Christ who died for all and offers peace with God, the peace which is the basic condition for peace among people and with creation.

These persons and such communities will be able to place *signposts* of reconciliation in church life, among mission movements, but also in the world of culture, economy and politics, including our relations to creation, on humanity's journey towards a future of which we know nothing, but in which we hope that unity and peace will prevail over judgement and enmity.

38 Robert Schreiter's books and papers are the essential reference for any reflection on a spirituality of reconciliation.

RECONCILING MISSION AND THE BODHISATTVA: NEVER DISPARAGING

Kenneth Fleming

We should not presume that God's mission of reconciliation falls foremost to Christians. In the context of contemporary political events, this paper explores what Christians might learn from an ancient Buddhist story of reconciling mission.

I begin, though, with a quite different narrative related to mission. This first story comes from the war in Iraq and tells us of its cost to one family. It has come to warrant a small mention in the world's media – a footnote to suffering. It is linked to what George W Bush has called America's 'great mission'[1] to protect and promote freedom. The story is from a newspaper report filed in Baghdad by Suzanne Goldenberg, a correspondent of *The Guardian*. She writes:

> In two adjoining stalls of the casualty ward of Kindhi hospital, the main trauma centre of eastern Baghdad, a girl, long black plait held off her forehead by a red Alice band, was laid out beside her little brother. Their mother lay across the aisle, beige dress soaked in blood from hem to armpits. Another brother slumped on the floor, insensible to the fact that he was sitting in his mother's blood.
>
> A neighbour who had followed the family to hospital said the girl had been called Noor Sabah and was 12 years old… Her brother, Abdel Khader, who began the day neatly dressed in dark trousers and a check shirt, was four or five. When their two small corpses were loaded on to the same gurney to take them to the morgue, even the nurses were reduced to tears.

1 George W Bush, "National Security Policy of the United States: Foreword by President George W. Bush," Government department on-line; Available at http://www.state.gov/r/pa/ei/wh/15434.htm; Internet. Accessed 13 June 2003.

> The doctors turned to watch the small bodies pass, the best they could offer by way of a ceremony, and abandoned the mother, Wael Sabah, on her gurney. "She's fatal," said one. The doctors could do no more but watch her die.[2]

The Buddhist story, from their sacred scriptures, concerns a previous life of the Buddha as missionary monk called Never Disparaging. The text came to my attention several years ago when I lived with a Japanese Buddhist order. One day, when hitchhiking out of London with two Buddhist nuns and two monks, a van sped by as we waited at the roadside. As it passed, racist abuse was directed at the Buddhists and three or four cans of beer - still mostly full - were thrown out of the window. A few of us were hit and as I nursed my injured arm I turned to see the monks and nuns bowing to the van as it sped off, and as they bowed they chanted a blessing. Later that day I was pointed to the story of Never Disparaging, whose example the monastics were trying to follow. The story, told by the Buddha, takes place in the forgotten past during a time when religion and society had become corrupt. The Buddha said:

> Monks of overbearing arrogance exercised great authority and power. At this time there was a bodhisattva monk named Never Disparaging...This monk, whatever persons he happened to meet, whether monks, nuns, laymen or laywomen, would bow in obeisance to all of them and speak words of praise, saying, 'I have profound reverence for you, I would never dare treat you with disparagement or arrogance. Why? Because you are all practising the bodhisattva way and are certain to attain Buddhahood.'
>
> This monk did not devote his time to reading or reciting the scriptures, but simply went about bowing to people.
>
> Many years passed in this way, during which this monk was constantly subjected to curses and abuse. He did not give way to anger, however, but each time spoke the same

2 Suzanne Goldenberg, 'A picture of killing inflicted on a sprawling city – and it grew more unbearable by the minute,' *The Guardian Newspaper*, Wednesday 9 April (2003): 1.

> words, 'You are certain to attain Buddhahood.' When he spoke in this manner, some among the group would take sticks of wood or tiles and stones and beat and pelt him. But even as he ran away and took up his stance at a distance, he continued to call out in a loud voice, 'I would never dare disparage you, for you are all certain to attain Buddhahood!' And because he always spoke these words, the overbearingly arrogant monks, nuns, laymen and laywomen gave him the name Never Disparaging ... The people gibed at him, cursed and reviled him, but the bodhisattva Never Disparaging bore all this with patience.[3]

The Buddha goes on to say that at the point of death the monk received special insight and a teaching which he preached to people over many lifetimes. Eventually, he came to convert those who had formerly oppressed him.

The article in the *Guardian* newspaper reminds us of great and recent suffering caused by our own hands. This, similar stories, and allied casualties, are presented as the unfortunate but necessary cost of the 'great mission' to bring freedom and democracy to a world endangered by terrorism and ruthless tyrants. Suffering of the innocent, we are told, will be kept to a minimum by massive investment in smart bombs using the latest pinpoint technology. If we are to believe it, the family of Wael Sabah has died for the greater good of freedom, which the people of Iraq can now taste. The trouble is that in the light of my Christian faith, I cannot bring myself to believe this. And I despair at the Christian support for state violence. It is true that politicians have been careful to argue that the 'great mission' is not a fight between Christianity and Islam, but religion does play a part. George W Bush sees his leadership as guided by Christian faith. It is reported that 'prayer is a feature of meetings at the White House, with bible studies led by other cabinet members.'[4] In his State of the Union address, Bush claimed that liberty is not America's gift to the world but God's gift to humanity.[5] It is worth defending and it is worth promoting, if need be by the use of overwhelming military force.

---

3 Burton Watson (trans.), *The Lotus Sutra* (New York: Columbia University Press, 1993), 266-268. Full story can be found on pages 265-271.

4 Douglas Fraser, "The Burning Bush," *Life and Work* (June 2003): 26.

5 Office of the Press Secretary, "President delivers 'State of the Union' address, 18 January 2003." Government department on-line; Available at

Most Christian leaders in America and in this country opposed Operation Iraqi Freedom. If opinion polls are to be believed, however, a majority of Christians in the States supported war. Many Christians, not just Bush and Blair, have spoken of it as being a morally justifiable war. I believe that a fundamental problem for Christians is the fact that for centuries followers of Christ have supported recourse to war and approved violence. Today, few would support theologically the notion of a holy war, but the culture of the acceptance of violence runs deep in our churches. War, it is argued, is recognised by the bible as a means to overcome injustice; theologically, it is defended as necessary in the face of human sinfulness and evil. It comes as no surprise then that war is justifiable in the eyes of many Christians to protect the American way of life and bring liberation to the Iraqi people. A question haunts me: how can we overcome this culture of the acceptance of violence and its glorification even in our churches? Perhaps Buddhism can help us.

The story of Never Disparaging comes from the Lotus Sutra, one of Mahayana Buddhism's most influential scriptures.[6] The name of the monk describes his ethical behaviour and his way of engaging in mission, he is Never Disparaging. He is also called a bodhisattva. A bodhisattva is one who is on the path to becoming a Buddha; who is motivated by great compassion and takes a vow to relieve the suffering of all sentient beings in this world. In order to do this the bodhisattva cultivates what are known as the six perfections: generosity, morality, patience, joyous effort, concentration, and wisdom. The mission of Never Disparaging is rooted in this compassionate concern for others and shaped by the six virtues. In facing violence, in being abused and beaten, his response is non-violent. From his mouth come words of hope and compassion; he shows respect and concern to those who hate and revile him.

This mission of the bodhisattva stands in contrast to the 'great mission' led by the American administration and supported by the

---

htpp://whitehouse.gov/news/releases/2003/01/20030128-19.html; Internet. Accessed 18 June 2003.

6 According to Wing-tsit Chan, the Lotus Sutra has been 'the source of inspiration for Buddhist practice in the Far East for the last 1500 years.' In Michael Fuss, *Buddhavacana and Dei Verbum: a phenomenological and theological comparison of scriptural inspiration in the Saddharmapundarika Sutra and in the Christian Tradition* (Leiden: E J Brill, 1991), 29.

Blair government. For we have engaged in a mission that relies heavily on violence, which at times seems motivated by fear and is supported by arrogant words. Deeply shocked and hurt by the events of 9/11, America has embarked on a foreign policy that is explicit in its threat to use massive military hardware to protect its interests and meet perceived threats.

Throughout history Buddhists have fought in wars also. There have been attempts to provide a canonical and philosophical rationale for a 'just war'.[7] But these attempts have mostly failed and a pan-Buddhist justification for war has never been accepted. So a leading monk, Santikaro Bhikku, can write:

> 'Just War' is an Oxymoron…. [It] makes no sense in a tradition dedicated to moral decency, non-harming, compassion, and wisdom…. The ends, even when decent and just, never justify the violence of war…. It is never morally legitimate.[8]

There is no sustainable rationale for a just war in Buddhism. In a religion where the means and the end are understood to be inextricably bound together, it is incongruous that peace can be achieved by violence or that good can be achieved by even a 'necessary' evil. This does not mean that Buddhists abrogate their responsibility in the political sphere. Recent times have witnessed the development of Socially Engaged Buddhism, where Buddhists apply non-violent means to actively tackle social injustice and war.[9] Buddhist leaders like the Dalai Lama for the Tibetan people, Maha Ghosananda in Cambodia, and Aung San Suu Kyi in Burma, have espoused an active non-violent approach in the face of immense suffering. Christians could learn from this witness.

The non-violent approach of the bodhisattva Never Disparaging, then, lives on in Buddhism today. One of the fruits of

---

7 See, for example, the arguments in Sri Lankan Buddhism. Tessa Batholomeusz, "In defence of Dharma: Just-War ideology in Buddhist Sri Lanka," *Journal of Buddhist Ethics*. Journal on-line; Available at http://jbe.gold.ac.uk/6/bartho991.htm; Internet. Accessed 24 April 2003.

8 Santikaro Bhikkhu, *"Just War" is an Oxymoron*, Available at http://www.liberationpark.org/bpf/ jw_oxy.htm; Internet. Accessed on 16 June 2003.

9 For a Buddhist analysis of the conflict between America and Islamic fundamentalism see, David R Loy, "A New Holy War against Evil? A Buddhist Response," Available at http://www.isss.org/911/loy.htm; Internet. Accessed 10 June 2003.

interreligious dialogue between Christians and Buddhists, where we listen attentively to Buddhist teachings and learn from the Buddhist witness, is that we are challenged and helped to reassess the Christian recourse to violence. In the witness of Never Disparaging, and many other Buddhist figures, we see reflections of the passion of Christ; and Buddhism may help us to look again with new eyes at the meaning of Christ's life, his passion and death. This would be in some ways to discover nothing new; for centuries the small, historic peace churches of the Mennonites and Quakers have kept alive the prophetic voice of non-violence. Our 'great mission,' in the face of unparalleled human violence in today's world, may then be to discover the riches and costliness of non-violence. In this our Buddhist friends can help us. Buddhists, who for so long have been the objects of our missions, become friends in a common mission to bring about peace through living non-violently: a mission that not only helps to bring reconciliation between peoples but also to a closer relationship with God.

As well as the general commitment to non-violence, Buddhism offers other tools for the overcoming of conflict and realisation of peace. For example, Buddhism is known for the attention it gives to the interior workings of the mind and for the need to develop mindfulness in all we do. It is concerned with the various causes and conditions that give rise to how people act. It stresses that in order to build world peace, people must overcome the sources of violence within – the greed, attachments, and delusions that cause selfishness and promote simplistic worldviews where we, all too quickly, divide peoples into good and evil. There is recognition that religion can be a force to liberate people or it can be a force to enslave people's minds. Here we can learn much from Buddhism in its concern to look within in order to bring transformation outwith; and in its refusal to demonise those who are different, whether in the political sphere or the missionary field.

Buddhism, like Christianity, is a missionary religion. The Buddha, out of great compassion, sent his followers to spread his teaching, the Dharma, to heal and to liberate. Never Disparaging is a missionary in this manner, a figure of self-giving whose witness and courage has been compared to that of Stephen in the Acts of the Apostles.[10] He comes across as someone with a generosity of heart. In Asia, Buddhists have often been critical of Christian

10 Fuss, *Buddhavacana and Dei Verbum*, 430.

missions for lacking this generosity of heart. When working as a missionary in Thailand, I entered into dialogue with a Buddhist monk. After overcoming initial suspicions, he told me how he felt about Christianity – he claimed that missionaries were conditioned by arrogance and by fear of the religious 'other' which led them to condemn Buddhism. He also accused Christians of using fear to coerce people into faith by stressing how they were doomed to eternal suffering because of their wrong beliefs. Christianity, in his eyes, was a religion of force that lacked humility and did violence to the sincerely held beliefs of others. Is there a link here with the violence we sanction in war? I am reminded of the comment of Kosuke Koyama, who claimed that Buddhists were introduced not to 'Christ crucified' but to 'Christ crucifying.'[11] We have operated in Asia with underlying theologies of mission and other religions that view people as little more than objects of conquest. We can learn from Never Disparaging that we cannot hope to touch the lives of people unless we do so with humility and generosity of heart.

To finish with, one other aspect of the story of Never Disparaging that Christians perhaps can learn from. The way in which he lived and witnessed is understood in Buddhism as encapsulating the truth he preached. His message of 'You are all to become buddhas' is authentic because he lives it. In Buddhism, the message of liberation is only meaningful when it is lived – right views and right livelihood belong together. In Christian theology and missions the impression is often given that having the right belief is more important than having the right livelihood. In this view truth and salvation are evidenced more in dogma, confession and church membership than through ethical behaviour. Belief comes before morality in the order of our loves. So when confronted with acts of self-sacrifice and compassion in Buddhists these can be dismissed as theologically deficient, or seen as a marker for a contest where we say we must be able to do better than them. I appreciate the emphasis in Buddhism that the truth is essentially ethical in nature and not derived, and that its focus is on the actual suffering of people. So I find myself more at home with Buddhist friends who sincerely struggle to overcome the three Buddhist poisons of greed, hatred and delusion than I often do with

11 Kosuke Koyama, *No Handle on the Cross: An Asian Meditation on the Crucified Mind* (London: SCM Press, 1976), 109.

Christian friends whose consuming concern is to convert others or who sit easily with condoning violence.

In Buddhism we may struggle to find the term reconciliation. But we see in the person of the bodhisattva Never Disparaging someone who strives for reconciliation. The spirituality of great compassion and self-giving that is captured for us in the cross are not new to Buddhism. There is a mission incumbent upon us all, I believe, to break down the barriers of distrust and hatred that separate us from learning from other religions. Such learning can lead us into a deeper understanding of our own faith and provide a powerful witness in the struggle for justice. For many centuries our disdain for other religions has prevented Christians from learning from them; now though, as ecumenism has grown, so has our willingness to listen and learn from others and once forbidden treasures become known to us.

References

Batholomeusz, Tessa. "In defence of Dharma: Just-War ideology in Buddhist Sri Lanka." *Journal of Buddhist Ethics*. Journal on-line. Available at http://jbe.gold.ac.uk/6/ bartho991.htm; Internet. Accessed 24 April 2003.

Bush, George W. "National Security Policy of the United States: Foreword by President George W. Bush." Government department on-line. Available from http://www.state.gov/ r/pa/ei/wh/15434.htm; Internet. Accessed 13 June 2003.

Dalai Lama, *The Good Heart*, London: Rider Books, 1997.

Fraser, Douglas. "The Burning Bush." *Life and Work* (June 2003): 24-27.

Fuji, Nichidatsu. *Fusessho (Non-Killing)*. Tokyo: Nipponzan Myohoji, 1985.

Fuss, Michael. *Buddhavacana and Dei Verbum: a phenomenological and theological comparison of scriptural inspiration in the Saddharmapundarika Sutra and in the Christian Tradition.* Leiden: E J Brill, 1991.

Goldenberg, Suzanne. 'A picture of killing inflicted on a sprawling city – and it grew more unbearable by the minute.' *The Guardian*, Wednesday 9 April (2003): 1.

Kim, Young-ho. *Tao-Sheng's Commentary on the Lotus Sutra: a study and translation.* Albany: State University of New York Press, 1990.

Koyama, Kosuke. *No Handle on the Cross: An Asian Meditation on the Crucified Mind.* London: SCM Press, 1976.

Loy, David R. "A New Holy War against Evil? A Buddhist Response." Available at http://www.isss.org/911/loy.htm; Internet. Accessed 10 June 2003.

Office of the Press Secretary. "President delivers 'State of the Union' address, 18 January 2003." Government department on-line. Available at htpp://whitehouse.gov/news/ releases/2003/01/20030128-19.html; Internet. Accessed 18 June 2003.

Santikaro Bhikkhu. "'Just War" is an Oxymoron." Available at http://www.liberationpark. org/bpf/jw_oxy.htm; Internet. Accessed on 16 June 2003.

Thich Nhat Hahn. *Being Peace*. London: Rider, 1987.

Watson, Burton (trans.). *The Lotus Sutra*. New York: Columbia University Press, 1993.

INTER RELIGIOUS DIALOGUE, CONFLICT AND RECONCILIATION

Andrew Wingate

It is easy to understand the now fashionable activity known as Inter Religious Dialogue as something comfortable, full of the discovery of what is common and harmonious. It can seem an easy road, exciting because, at least in the west, it is something new. Theological motivation may come out of a pluralist ideology. Differences may be there, but since we are each on different paths up the mountain, or on different spokes of a wheel, there is no reason for these to lead to conflict. At its best, this kind of dialogue can lead to a sharing of spiritual experience, where each can cross over to the other, and important things be discovered by both of us. Doctrine is better avoided, and we search rather for a common ethic, as well as a common spirituality.

This is one side of inter faith dialogue, and it centres on the essential principle that 'dialogue begins when people meet people.' This is the first of four principles of inter faith dialogue, as agreed by the British churches in the 1980's, based upon the World Council of Churches work in this area. These have stood the test of time, and though they are under review from several directions at the time of writing, I believe they can still provide a very useful framework for balanced engagement across faiths. But there is another side to the enterprise, as suggested by the second principle, 'dialogue depends upon removing misunderstanding and building up trust.' Only if this stage has been addressed, is it easy to move to the last two principles, 'dialogue leads to common service to the community', and 'dialogue is a means of authentic witness.' As the Chief Rabbi, Jonathan Sacks, has now famously written, in his book *The Dignity of Difference* (Continuum, 2002), religions are either part of the problem of this world, or they are part of the solution to those problems. This means addressing very seriously the second principle above. In a different field, the explosion of problems related to the debate on homosexuality in the Anglican Church, which we are at present experiencing, arises from a situation where there is little trust between evangelicals and liberals, between Africans, Europeans and Americans. Hence it is difficult to move towards any action, which can be sustained, for the benefit of the whole church. There can be no real critique of the different positions, because there is no real listening.

In the field of inter religious encounter, I will illustrate these issues of misunderstanding, conflict and reconciliation largely through my experience of initiating, leading and participating in dialogue programmes in the last three years, since I have been in Leicester. It depends greatly which religions are involved, and I will therefore write about particular examples.

Context also matters greatly, and therefore the reader needs a few statistics about Leicester. It is a city of 279,000 in the East Midlands of England. The census of 2001 revealed that 36% of the population are not of European origin. The majority of these are of Indian background, with more than 31,000 Muslims, 41,000 Hindus, and 10,000 Sikhs within the city boundaries, discounting those who live just outside, and those who either declare no religion or do not register, perhaps because they are asylum seekers. Jews are now no more than 500 people. Christians are nominally 42%, clearly only a minority being church attenders.

Muslim-Christian Dialogue

This is the most common form of dialogue world-wide, which is not surprising, because these are the two main missionary religions, which now exist in almost every country of the globe. They therefore come into close contact, for good or ill. In countries such as Northern Nigeria or Sudan, there is likely to be little dialogue because there is no basic trust that such will not be exploited for political reasons. But in other African countries such as Tanzania, Ghana or Sierra Leone, Muslims and Christians work well together on common concerns, there is intermarriage without it being a great scandal, and there is a fair trust within the difficult economic and political realities of those places.

In both Birmingham and Leicester, I have initiated intentional dialogue groups. The one in Birmingham lasted about five years in the 1980's (as recorded in my book *Encounter in the Spirit, Muslim-Christian Dialogue in practice*, WCC, Risk Books, 1988, 1991). The Leicester group has now been running for two and a half years, and has given birth to a separate women's dialogue group. The contexts are similar and different.

In Birmingham we were involved with Sufi Muslims. This enabled trust to grow more quickly, with the ability before long to pray alongside each other, and indeed together. Crucial occasions for growth were when as Christians we gave full support to the Muslim members, after two Muslims were killed in disturbances in Handsworth. Memorable was my walking down Lozells High Street with the Muslim leader, hand in hand with his young daughter, as houses smouldered around us after widespread arson attacks, as an expression of solidarity. Another was when we faced potential polarisation, with the first Gulf War, in 1990. We held three hours of readings and prayer, as the United Nations deadline passed and the bombers prepared to take off. So also, when the Babri mosque was destroyed, we held a meeting for all faiths, when we lit candles, expressed our feelings in mixed groups, read from scriptures and prayed in quiet. These actions in face of conflict depended upon prior knowledge of each other, friendship and trust. This came from meeting monthly over a long period, and much hard work.

In Leicester, we have faced several conflicts together. They have included the Gujarat religious strife in 2002, which resulted in the deaths of 2000 Muslims, the ongoing anguish of the Holy Land, and wars in Afghanistan and Iraq. More domestic issues include that at present related to controversy around Halal meat, and the possibility of BNP marches in Leicester (consequently banned by the police). We have been able to hold together through all these, to discuss them in depth, and to hold public meetings of solidarity. We have also raised about £12,000 for common causes-for Save the Children in Afghanistan, and a joint fund for a Christian hospital in Gaza and a Muslim project in Kosovo. Each community entrusted their money jointly. Most important of all, after 9/11, at our Faith Leaders' Meeting, we affirmed a doctrine that an attack on one of us would be treated as an attack upon us all, and we were not prepared to allow local Muslims to be scapegoated, for what had happened in the USA. I personally wrote a long article on 'Muslims who have spoken against terrorism', in answer to an article in the Church of England Newspaper, 'Why will Muslims not speak out against terrorism.' This was much appreciated by Muslims, and I used quotations from local Muslims and also from a challenging publication, over

250 pages long '*The Quest for Sanity- reflections on September 11th and the aftermath,* from the Muslim Council of Britain.

In our regular group meetings, we have discussed contentious theological issues- is Mohammed a prophet? What is our understanding of revelation? Of God? Of Christ? So also social issues have been addressed such as the position of women, and the contentious themes of religious education, and faith schools. On religious education we were addressed by two members of the group, one who is a Muslim head of RE in a Church secondary school, the other a Christian who is head of RE in a state school which is 90% Muslim. In terms of potential conflict, high on the list have been discussions about mission and conversion. We have not only discussed these academically, but heard from converts from both sides. It is not easy for Christians to hear why someone has become a Muslim, but far more trust is needed for a Christian who was formerly a Muslim to speak in an audience including Muslims. But respect was maintained on these evenings, as we struggled to understand the life journeys that were articulated. We have also discussed racism, as we considered how to prevent in Leicester the kind of riots experienced in northern cities in 2001. This discussion did not become an attack on white Christians. Indeed a Muslim lay person challenged us to acknowledge that we are racist in some way or another. An Imam added that he wished to challenge his Muslim colleagues, 'Why did we not welcome the Somalis to Leicester, in the way that we welcomed the Bosnians? Was it because one group was black and the other white?'

The above account shows what can be achieved if sufficient time has been given for trust to develop. Potential conflicts can be faced and trust built up further, leading to common action. Key also is hard work put in between meetings, particularly between leaders. Such groups are normally based on very particular friendships, such as I have had with three Muslims, an Imam, a lay person and an academic, and which other Christians also have experienced. A final example of this trust was a journey that three of us Anglican clergy made by coach to the vast demonstration against the potential war against Iraq in February 2003. The coach was organised by Muslims. We received great courtesy all day, and participated in numerous informal dialogues. On the return journey food was shared with us from all sides of the coach, and I felt a deep sense of gratefulness from them that we had been there for them. Hence, as we ate together, I felt a sense of 'the sacramental', if not 'the sacrament'.

Family of Abraham Group

This was formed between Muslims, Jews and Christians, in 2002. The Israeli ambassador had visited Leicester and I was invited to bring Christian colleagues to meet him. I replied that I would do this, if I could bring a group of Muslims as well. He agreed to this, and we had a forthright, but respectful and honest discussion about Palestine. The ambassador invited us to visit the Holy Land together, to verify some of the areas of dispute. But the ground situation, and the lack of established trust in our Leicester group has so far precluded this.

We decided to spend time getting to know each other in Leicester. Whenever Palestine was discussed in any detail, differences and mistrust quickly arose. I therefore ruled out of order that subject, until we had grown to trust each other more. We had very helpful visits to each other's places of worship, and I thought trust was growing, as Jews found themselves welcomed in a mosque- the first time most of them had been there- and witnessed the prayers and the warmth of the community. This was reciprocated in both church and synagogue.

However, the situation remained fragile. Unfortunately, a reporter from the *Jewish Chronicle* came recently to Leicester to interview members of the group. She reported very well on the favourable situation in Leicester for the Jewish community, and commended our group. However, one sentence stood out in a contrary way. A particular Progressive Jew, one of the most dialogical of people and a pillar of the Council of Faiths, as well as of this dialogue group, was quoted as saying that Muslims he knew were very good in Leicester, with the exception of those connected with an organisation based in the city, called 'Friends of Al Aqsa'. This *de facto* called for ethnic cleansing of Jews from Israel. He was unaware that most Muslims in Leicester, including key members of our group, are in this organisation, and one is the Secretary. In no time, there were 62 e-mails to the Council of Faiths, from indignant Muslims, and the threat of a libel action.

I was asked by both communities to chair a meeting in the church hall, considered a neutral venue, to talk things through, as well as being asked to draft a reply to the e mails. We had an hour and a half of very tough talking. In the end the Progressive Jewish friend affirmed he was prepared to withdraw his statement, in the terms he had expressed it, and wrote to the *Jewish Chronicle* accordingly. I hoped that this would be the end of it, and we made a plan for further meetings of the group on 'neutral subjects'. But I found that the next regular meeting we had could not address the subject we had planned, as feelings resurfaced, and we talked it through again.

Relationships, however, remain good, and I hope and pray, that after a summer break, in the autumn we may be able to move forward, chastened but in touch with the reality of our feelings. Ironically, in the midst of all this, Muslims and Jews have been able to support each other in their thinking about Halal/Kosher meat, where issues are common, and the securing of proper burial facilities for the two communities. As Christians we have been called upon to support them both.

In general here, we have faced the conflict, and are in a period when we wait to see whether there can be real reconciliation, and building of trust. A hopeful sign is that both the Secretary of Al Aqsa, and the President of the Synagogue have offered to resign from the group, if it will help the rest to continue. I hope neither will leave.

Hindu-Christian Dialogue Groups

I am involved with two Hindu-Christian groups, and they have followed different patterns. Nationally, I am co-chair of the Hindu-Christian Forum of UK. This was formed about two years ago, and we began by considering areas of difficulty between us. Immediately prominent was the difficult issue of mission and conversion. This agenda came, before we knew each other, yet alone trusted each other. We proceeded over several meetings to try to agree a common statement, in an area which has divided Christians and Hindus since Gandhi's time at least, with his deep suspicion of Christian mission. This has recently become far more high profile, with Hindutva ideology now so strong in India, and the BJP government in power in Delhi.

We went through a tortuous process of drafting and redrafting seemingly endlessly. When we seemed to have got near agreement, from the Christian side we experienced new Hindus coming to the meeting, and blocking things, by introducing fresh issues. In the end we had to suspend the meeting for six months.

We jointly agreed that only named members should come, only two from any one Hindu or Muslim organisation. We then had a positive meeting, where we began again by considering positive stories of co-operation, arising from our local contexts. At our recent meeting, we were able at last to agree quite a significant statement about conversion, and agree that it was for the UK and not for India. Even at this meeting, there were attempts from the Hindu side to remove particular words or *de facto* to rule out even genuine conversion. However, by allowing all to have their say, and by agreeing to one or two small changes, we were able to complete the statement. Christians adhered to what they felt was a fundamental freedom to change faith, while Hindus felt that their concerns about pressured conversions were heard and included. It was important here to remember the rules of conflict resolution, that we should seek a 'win-win' situation, and in the end all felt they had won something.

At the local level, we have run a very different group, started a year ago, with the help of the Teape Foundation, established in Cambridge for encouraging Christian-Hindu dialogue in India. India has now come to Leicester! We meet for a meal, in a temple or church, have prayer, and then discuss agreed topics, arising from a joint planning group. These topics have tended to be of an undivisive kind; festivals and our understanding of God, mysticism and prayer, non-violence, mixed marriages. There has been a good atmosphere, and we have been getting to know each other well, and to respect each other. We have not yet tackled the difficult issues- such as mission, caste, racism etc. This is an alternative model to the other group above.

What is clear from both these groups, is that we are in a very different world from the Muslim-Christian-Jewish world. It is east meeting west, different kinds of religions meeting, with different sets of agendas. It is also a dialogue with polite and gentle people, but underneath there are very real agendas. These are harder to reach than with the 'religions of the book.', in my experience.

Muslim-Hindu Dialogue

As a result of the above groups, a Muslim approached me one day, and sought my advice in establishing a Muslim-Hindu group. I suggested whom he could contact, to enable a good beginning. Suspicions are many, not least because of the deeply divisive Gujarat situation, and Kashmir. Since most of Leicester's 36%

non-white population is Gujarati Hindu or Muslim, this is right at the heart of potential conflict. So far, they have only met to decide the agenda. Rightly they have said that it will be a confidential meeting, without allowing the media to be reporting on it. At the height of the Gujarat crisis, the Muslims had called an open meeting; 40 or so Muslims came, 6 Christians, and only one Hindu. Now at least they are beginning to talk together. Here the problem is not that of not knowing each other; they have lived happily in the city together for years. But it is a breakdown of trust, such as we have also seen on a bigger scale within the settled communities of the former Yugoslavia.

Final thoughts

Clearly there are parts of the world where inter religious dialogue at times of conflict has become a matter of life or death. Kaduna in Nigeria, Palestine, Burma, Sri Lanka would be examples. But here in Britain, we have a chance to enable a model for Europe and further afield. Our relatively free context can enable us to meet without fear of being misunderstood, except, in each case, by our own more conservative colleagues. Our very engagement in dialogue may bring us into conflict with our own people. Here comes the need for education of our own communities, and I have been much involved in that. But at their best, these dialogue groups have enabled conflicts to be faced, and struggles to be faced together. They have provided examples of what St Paul has called 'the ministry of reconciliation' that is at the heart of the Christian gospel, but also at the centre of each of these religions in their core. 'Loving our neighbour' does not mean agreeing with each other, but respecting each other and what each believes, with our differences. As Rowan Williams put it in his recent keynote lecture on the relationship between Christians and people of other faiths, delivered at Birmingham University, dialogue is important, as we learn to search for truth, to acknowledge our differences, and to rejoice in how we handle those differences. Such a description of dialogue summarises what we have discovered in the encounters described in this article.

SELECT BIBLIOGRAPHY

Mohammed Abu-Nimer: *Reconciliation, Co-Existence and Justice in Interethnic Conflict (*New York: Lexington Books, 2001)

Mohammed Abu-Nimer: *Non-Violence and Peace Building in Islam* (Granville, F L: University of Florida Press, 2003)

R Scott Appleby: *The Ambivalence of the Sacred: Religion, Violence and Reconciliation* (Oxford: Rowman and Littlefield, 2000)

S Bevans, E Doidge, R Schreiter (eds): *The Healing Circle: Essays in Cross Cultural Mission* (Chicago: CCGM Publications, 2000)

F Boal, M Keane, D Livingstone: *Them and Us* (Belfast: Institute of Irish Studies, 1997)

J G Bock: *Sharpening Conflict Movement: Religious Leadership and the Double-Edged Sword* (Westport C T: Praegar, 2001)

A Borine, J Levy, R Scheffer (eds): *Dealing with the Past; Truth and Reconciliation in South Africa* (Capetown: IDASA, 1994)

D Bosch: *Transforming Mission: Paradigm Shifts in the Theology of Mission* (Orbis, 1991)

S Bruce: *God Save Ulster* (Oxford: OUP, 1986)

Caritas: *Peacebuilding: A Caritas Training Manual* (Vatican City: Caritas Internationalist, 2002)

M A Cejka, T Bamat (eds): *Artisans of Peace: Grassroots Peacemaking Among Christian Communities* (Orbis, 2003)

Cecelia Clegg and Joseph Liechty: *Moving Beyond Sectarianism: Religious Conflict and Reconciliation in Northern Ireland* (Dublin: Columba Press, 2001)

John de Gruchy: *Reconciliation: Restoring Justice* (London: SCM Press, 2002)

G de Schrijver: *Liberation Theologies on Shifting Grounds* (Leuven: Uitgeverij Peeters, 1998)

M Dillon: *God and the Gun* (Belfast: Orion, 1997)

J Dunlop: *A Precarious Belonging: Presbyterians and Conflict in Ireland* (Belfast: Blackstaff Press, 1995)

A Falconer and J Liechty (eds): *Reconciling Memories* (Dublin: Columba Press, 1998)

M Fuss: *Buddhavacana and Dei Verbum* (Leiden: E J Brill, 1991)

A Gittins: *Reading the Clouds: Mission Spirituality for New Times* (Ligouri Publications, 2000)

C Gunton (ed): *The Theology of Reconciliation* (London: T & T Clark, 2003)

David Hempton: *Religion and Political Culture in Britain and Ireland* (CUP, 1996)

G L Higgins: *The Hard Gospel* (Dublin: Church of Ireland, 2003)

M Hill: *The Time of the End* (Belfast: Belfast Society, 2001)

G Jordan: *Not of this World* (Belfast: Blackstaff Press, 2001)

K Koyama: *No Handle on the Cross: An Asian Meditation on the Crucified Mind* (SCM Press, 1976)

J P Lederach: *The Journey Towards Reconciliation* (Scottdale P A: Herald Press, 1999)

J P Lederach: *Building Peace* (Washington: US Institute for Peace, 1997)

A E Lewis: *Between Cross and Resurrection: A Theology of Holy Saturday* (Grand Rapids: Eerdmans, 2001)

L J Luzbetak: *The Church and Culture* (Techny I L: Divine Word Publications, 1963)

F Lyons: *Ireland Since the Famine* (London: Fontana, 1973)

F Macpherson: *North of the Zambezi: A Modern Missionary Memoir* (Edinburgh: The Handsel Press, 1998)

J McCracken: *Politics and Christianity in Malawi 1875-1940* (CUP, 1977)

S C Neill: *A History of Christian Missions* (London: Pelican, 1964)

Norman Porter: *The Elusive Quest* (Belfast: Blackstaff, 2003)

M Reilly: *Spirituality for Mission: Historical, Theological and Cultural Factors for Present Day Missionary Spirituality* (Orbis, 1978)

Kenneth Ross: *Christianity in Malawi: A Sourcebook (*Gweru: Mambo Press, 1996)

Robert Schreiter: *Reconciliation: Mission and Ministry in a Changing Social Order* (Orbis, 1992)

C Schrock-Shenk (ed): *Meditation and Facilitation Training Manual: Foundations and Skills for Constructive Conflict Transformation* (Akron, P A: Mennonite Conciliation Service, 2000)

Peter Taylor: *The Brits: The War Against the IRA* (Bloomsbury, 2002)

Thich Nhat Hanh: *Being Peace* (Berkeley: Parallax Books, 1987)

A Thompson (ed): *Faith in Ulster* (Belfast: ECONI, 1996)

A Thompson (ed): *The Great White Tent* (Belfast: ECONI, 1999)

Desmond Tutu: *No Future Without Forgiveness* (London: Rider, 1999)

C Villa-Vicencio: *A Theology of Reconstruction: Nation Building and Human Rights* (CUP, 1992)

Miroslav Volf: *Exclusion and Embrace: A Theological Exploration of Identity, Otherness and Reconciliation* (Nashville: Abingdon, 1996)

B Watson (translator): *The Lotus Sutra* (New York: Columbia University Press, 1993)

ISBN 1 898362 25 4

2000

MISSION
and SPIRITUALITY
CREATIVE WAYS OF BEING CHURCH

Edited by

Howard Mellor & Timothy Yates

Papers by David Hay, Saunders Davies, Robert Kaggwa, Brian Stanley, Pete Ward, Laurenti Magesa, Michael Crowley, Esther de Waal, John Burgess, Craig Gardiner

How will the church be shaped to meet the needs of the 21st century? In this collection, contributors from Britain, Tanzania, Uganda and Latin America reflect on creative ways of being church in the challenging contexts of post-modern society: and on what can be learned from the spiritual traditions of the past to provide an inner dynamic matched to the future.

'This collection is better than a curate's egg: all the parts are good .... a thought provoking "must-have" for all who share passion for mission and evangelism of any kind today' *Anvil*

CLIFF COLLEGE PUBLISHING

ISBN 1 898362 28 9

2002

A companion volume to

MISSION – AN INVITATION TO GOD'S FUTURE

and

MISSION – VIOLENCE AND RECONCILIATION